LIFE LESSONS IN CUSTOM CHARTER AVIATION

Tailor-Made to Fly

TRACEY DEAKIN

With Dawn C. Crouch

HELLGATE PRESS   ASHLAND, OREGON

TAILOR-MADE TO FLY
Life Lessons in Custom Charter Aviation
©2024 Tracey Deakin

Published by Hellgate Press
(An imprint of L&R Publishing, LLC)

Hellgate Press
2305 Ashland St., #104-176
Ashland, OR 97520
email: sales@hellgatepress.com

Cover and Interior Design: L. Redding

*Cover photos of Tracey Deakin courtesy of
David Hammond Brown Photography
(davidhammondbrown.com)*

ISBN: 978-1-954163-88-1

Library of Congress Control Number: 2024945373

First edition 10 9 8 7 6 5 4 3 2 1

This is my true story, as far as I can recollect. I have followed up to make sure the events and persons depicted are as accurate as possible, but still reflect within the prism of time and personal experience. I have worked hard, been extremely fortunate, and it is my intention to encourage young aviators and honor those giants in aviation and aerospace that I met and worked with along the way.

— TD

Life's inspirations are little gifts along the way.
With sincerity, I acknowledge the following
in support of this memoir:

Jim Deakin

Ted Cooper

Brian Mansfield

Gerry Bron

Phil Battaglia

Ken Haas

Mike Whitman

Judith Menichello

Dawn Crouch

Guy Norris

Dave Krisanda

Wing Commander Hugh Charles Kennard DFC

For my wife and family

Tailor-Made to Fly

Contents

Tailor-Made to Fly

Foreword

P EOPLE IN THE AVIATION business, perhaps like no other, are filled with passion and enthusiasm for what they do, and Tracey Deakin is one of those individuals.

Since encountering Tracey's remarkable "can-do" attitude for the first time more than thirty years ago, I have witnessed him use these innate qualities to help pilot a fledgling aviation charter company from the ground up into a leading global organization.

Telling the story of his aviation roots and the growth of Le Bas International in his own inimitable style, Tracey gives us not only a blueprint for how to build and manage a successful aviation business but also a glimpse into the vanished golden era of early large jet and turboprop air cargo operations in Europe and Africa.

Ranging from adventures carrying cargoes of calves over the Alps in temperamental Bristol Britannia freighters during his early days at Invicta International Airlines — a long vanished British charter carrier — to dangerous flights to Africa in elderly Douglas DC-8s, Tracey's tales recall an almost totally forgotten "tramp steamer" age of the aviation business.

Following a roundabout course through flying stints in the British Channel Islands and Datapost in the UK, Tracey then tells us about his unplanned entre to executive aviation and the start of his journey into managing corporate and private charters.

After formative experiences with operators ranging from El Al to Zambia Airways, Tracey's big break comes in the late 1980s with a typically Deakin "he who dares wins" move to the U.S.A. and the start of a love affair with America which lasts to this day.

Working his way into operations in California with the start-up Le Bas company, Tracey's story recounts exhausting round-the-clock days to establish credibility and carve out a niche in a highly competitive landscape.

Soaring to new heights, he recounts the company's early major charter achievements like organizing the world tour for British band Pink Floyd, Hollywood "A-listers" and other celebrities.

But while passion and enthusiasm can carry you through a lot, the real test is often how you react when things go wrong. In December 1993 Tracey faced just such a test when a Le Bas chartered aircraft carrying Rich Snyder and other executives of the In-N-Out burger chain company crashed on approach to John Wayne-Orange County Airport in California.

The IAI Westwind was returning Snyder and his group from opening the 93rd In-N-Out restaurant in Fresno but was tragically caught in the wake of a United Airlines Boeing 757 on the approach to the airport. Although tracking the instrument landing system on a normal glideslope and following standard separation procedures, the Westwind suddenly flew into the ground around four miles from the runway, killing all aboard.

Investigations soon showed that the aircraft hit the wake of the 757 when it was two miles in trail and 400 ft. below the United airliner.

Shocked to the core by the event, Tracey led efforts to change standards under which some aircraft are separated from each other on final approach.

At the time I witnessed first-hand Tracey's determination to get at the wake turbulence problem as I helped with his research into the existing standards and with writing letters to the FAA.

As a result of this accident, as well as several similar events between 1983 and 1993, the U.S. National Transportation Safety Board (NTSB), conducted a special investigation that resulted in wake turbulence being added to what the NTSB called its "Most Wanted" list of safety concerns in 1995.

Tracey's actions, amongst others, helped prompt the FAA into a series of improvements — critically including more spacing behind 757s — and wake turbulence was removed from the Most Wanted list in 1998.

The "In-N-Out" accident began an industry changing phase of research and additional safety procedures to prevent similar incidents from occurring again, and it also put renewed energy into Tracey's passion for improved operational safety.

Le Bas developed the Air Carrier's Commercial Operating Manual to help maintain higher standards and promoted safety rules and requirements that are now codified into U.S. Department of Transport regulations for air charter companies.

Beyond the critical aspect of safety, Tracey's inspirational charter story also embraces a vast range of experiences from organizing humanitarian aid and disaster relief missions to helping with movie shoots and flying large groups to remote islands to witness rocket launches.

Whether he's dispensing lessons on how to treat customers, improving safety or simply amusing us with anecdotes, the bottom line is Tracey's aviation life has — and continues to be — fueled by passion and an infectious enthusiasm that leaps out at you from these pages.

Tracey is also irrepressibly positive and through his story reminds us that both optimists and pessimists contribute to our society. In particular — to use the well-known quote, as applied to aviation — the optimist invents the airplane and the pessimist the parachute.

Guy Norris, Colorado Springs, Colorado, USA
January 2023

CHAPTER 1

Tailor-Made to Fly

*"Lovers of air travel find it exhilarating to hang poised between
the illusion of immortality and the fact of death."*

— Alexander Chase

I N MY MIND, AVIATION and aerospace are magic. I'm Tracey
Deakin, a founding partner of Le Bas International, one of the
world's premier private air charter companies, and I stand on the
magic of history. People, destinations, the Wright Brothers, technology, everyone who got us to where we are today.

I never forget where it all started, where it all came from because
if it wasn't for all those pioneers of industry — KLM, Silver City,
Imperial Airways (before British Airways), and Pan Am — I wouldn't
be here, and we wouldn't be having this conversation.

In the early days of air travel, passengers had to be enticed to board
an airplane. Flying was high adventure, a risky undertaking. Plane
travel was pretty frightening. They were going up in these jalopies
that were tied together by string, paper, and canvas, but they did it.

Commercial plane travel progressed, and as more people traveled,
competition flourished because air travel became safer. At least,
that's what we tell ourselves.

But when you really think about it, airplanes are like leopards.
They're very beautiful. Totally exquisite. They're a work of science
and technology, even a work of art, but if you get them on a wrong
day, that claw will take your face off.

So initially, the only way to get people on board was to offer an experience.

People were enticed by hospitality and comfort. Stewardesses were uniformly beautiful, and stewards dressed up like butlers. The initial way airlines attracted passengers was to offer first-class service. But excellent customer amenities needed one more tangible benefit to allow commercial air travel to take off. Pun intended.

What was the real value offered by aviation? One word: Speed.

Travel time from London to Paris was cut from a day and a half to one hour and forty-five minutes.

Tech is clinical. Tech is state of the art. Tech has no character. Technology drives innovation.

But last I looked, we are human beings, and we need hugs, smiles, and pleasantries. Technology is good, but not at the expense of human interaction. Think back to early cross-country train travel in America. Pretty wild. You could get stranded, held up, whatever, but the lure for passengers was to offer upper-end service.

People used to get on ocean liners to come across to America. It would take four or five days to do that, but it was the quickest, most straightforward way to travel the distance at that time. So, what are all the passengers going to do in these ocean liners?

The cruise lines created the means for social interaction. Passengers could meet other passengers. They offered dancing and a theater. They prepared elaborate and delicious food onboard. Otherwise, the passengers were not going to get on the ship. What if the owners had said, "We're going to float you across the Atlantic, and we're only going to give you a sandwich?"

That's not going to happen.

Rich people are often the first to try new technologies. Why? The wealthy travel in style because they have the money to do it. Why is Richard Branson doing what Richard Branson is doing? Because he has the money, but he also has the desire to make it happen. He has the means to make his vision realized. But notice that he's working with other people all the time to create opportunities, community, and jobs. All because of Richard's initial ambition and imagination.

If it weren't for the visionary, the secondary would never happen. Now, people get on commercial airplanes with chips and sandwiches. They sit down, and boom, they're fast asleep! For most people, traveling on an aircraft is no longer an experience. It's more like a bus service, and most people dread it.

On my end of the business, as a purveyor of aircraft charter, we still provide that original high standard of service. The one constant about aviation, about aerospace, is innovation, and it's wonderful. There's not a single day that you don't get up and somebody has invented something new and different. So many people all around the world are innovators. But again, I believe the most important thing is the client.

I think of the influence of my father. As his prodigy, I became the person I am. A salesman. I'm a purveyor of services. So, when something happens at Le Bas International, no matter if we're rescuing people, delivering goods, orchestrating a musical tour, carrying an elephant, or transporting someone in the public domain, I think, "Woohoo. Did it. That went well." And I feel a buzz. Always.

There's not a place on the planet we haven't been. We've had some of the most loved presidents, entertainers, sports personalities, and private individuals as guests, our customers, for the last five decades. I get a lot of satisfaction from a job well done. I think the buzz I feel is just the human condition celebrating itself and knowing it's shared something and done some good.

I was born in 1957. My parents were incredible people, but in the post-war United Kingdom, you were brought up to be the stiff upper lip, British gentleman. My father was just such a gentleman. He looked like David Niven, very suave, and absolute. As for me, when I was growing up, I was born with clubfeet. Nobody's fault. Genetics, that's just the way it was.

As I grew, I had to undergo orthopedic operations at progressive intervals. The Royal Sea Bathing Hospital in Margate was an old place, one of the first orthopedic hospitals in the world. The Quaker physician Dr. John Coakley Lettsom founded it on 2nd July 1791. The building was made of stone, not regimental, but ancient-looking. The grounds looked like something out of India, with big courtyards and grassy areas.

When I was three years old, I was a patient there for a good year. Both my feet were in plaster. My bones were broken, and I had steel things put through my toes to bring them out. I had a second operation when I was seven or eight, and that time, I was in the hospital for about eight months. As you get older and grow, the surgeons have to continually correct your bones. I had a third operation when I was about fourteen.

So, where am I going with this?

I was school age, and at that time, parents who wanted the very best for their children were expected to send them away for their education. When I was five, I went to boarding school, and I wasn't seen as exceptionally bright simply because I had spent so much time in hospital. I had ideas, but I couldn't excel. The reason was that I was absent from the classroom. I missed essential building blocks, so all the other kids were ahead of me. I was out of the curriculum. I was out of step with everybody else.

But in every negative, there's a positive, and I always look for the positive. I admit that it takes years of practice, years and years and years of practice to make your mind think like that.

At Bethany School in Goudhurst, Kent, I would sit on a wooden bench built around the trunk of a young oak tree beside the gymnasium on summer evenings. I felt the wind, listened to the stirrings of the leaves. In the distance, other students played football or studied for exams. I could see them, but my attention was elsewhere.

I watched the sky.

In the fading light of sunset, I would first hear the airplane, then see it descending, not fast but slow, with the power pulled back. Then, finally peeling off, the VC-10, arriving from wherever, would head toward London to land.

Where did the planes travel from? Where would they go next? I asked questions that took me outside of myself. I knew my limitations only too well, but these first experiences observing flight left a deep and lasting impression. There was a world outside of me, away from the hospital and apart from school.

I was seven years old when I went on my first solo flight to visit my sister. She was fourteen years my senior, and lived in Libya, just after Gaddafi assumed power.

As I boarded the plane, I was not treated as a child but as an honored guest. Taking my seat, I stared from the window at the myriad of blue lights striping the taxiway. Those blue lights shone over and above the dim overhead illumination inside the cabin.

When I used to watch the planes from my favorite bench at school, I had heard the sound of the plane's engines turning to land. But sitting inside the aircraft as a passenger, I felt the engines turning on the VC-10, and the sound surrounded me.

During the flight, I was invited into the cockpit, and I can still see the crew and instruments as clear as if I were standing there today, the co-pilot, the captain, and all these dials in front of them. I can picture the exact view looking out the cockpit window.

"Welcome aboard, young man. What are you doing? Where are you going?" The captain showed me around the cockpit and asked, "Would you like to do this one day?"

I replied without hesitation, "Wow. Can I stay?"

My break into aviation was born from my curiosity about Manston, the airport near my home. My family lived in Ramsgate, a small town on the southeastern coast of England, about one and a half hours from London.

Manston has a hundred-year-old history, but it is best remembered as a World War II airport in the Battle of Britain, and a big station for the U.S. Air Force. Imagine the airport, fresh from the second World War, built and maintained as a military installation. Manston was a massive airport with nine thousand sixteen feet of runway.

But just after the war, Manston wasn't busy at all. Airplanes used to come by, but fairly infrequently. On the weekends sometimes, it was totally quiet. A seagull making an approach on the runway was the important event of the day. It was like, "All right. Here we go. You can do it."

Invicta International operated out of Manston. The company had its own airplanes, the Bristol Britannia, or as they were called, the Whispering Giant of the 1950s, a lovely airplane. One of my favorites.

Hugh Kennard, the gentleman who started Invicta International, was Wing Commander Kennard during the Battle of Britain. He was in charge of the Polish Air Force, and those pilots were crazy flyers. He wanted them to be all together. Don't go anywhere you shouldn't. Don't take unnecessary risks. British, upper lip, remember? The only problem was that's not the way the Poles operated.

As soon as these pilots saw trouble, they would go after it like bees to honey.

"Guys, get back here!" Hugh Kennard would try his best to stop them.

They were like, "No! We need to be where the action is!" And they were off and gone, so he used to have to follow them, corral them all, and haul them back into formation again.

He was shot down three times and survived.

Before Hugh Kennard started Invicta International, he had a company called Silver City. He started Silver City with a gentleman by the name of Freddie Laker. He did a brilliant job at it, and the two were partners for a while before Hugh Kennard founded Invicta International and Freddie created Laker Airways. Laker Airways was the very first airline to operate DC-10s between London, Gatwick, and the States. He was the first to offer low-cost, get-on-an-airplane with service, back-and-forth to the United States.

I was fascinated by the Manston airport, but there was one slight problem.

I was meant to go into my father's business. I was supposed to be a tailor.

Deakin & Sons of Canterbury was founded by my great-grandfather in 1856. My father managed the two stores: one in Canterbury and the other in Ramsgate. My older brother went into the business.

In the last century, one of the most critical facts of everyday life was that everybody dressed in suits. Suits were king. It didn't matter what you did or who you were. Whether you were a Spivey, a cleaning person, a taxi driver, or a horseman, you were expected to dress properly in uniforms. At the time, suits were all handmade and considered an essential ingredient of a successful public persona. If you weren't dressing smart, you wouldn't be walking through the door.

The Ramsgate and Canterbury stores used to do a lot of business in aviation uniforms for pilots. My father fashioned a hat for me to the exact specifications of the ones made for the pilots for that first flight of mine. I wore my hat, complete with a pilot's badge on it, to fly that day.

The summer I was fifteen was idyllic. I had a canoe. I was down at Ramsgate Harbour every single day to take the canoe out in the ocean. Every single day, I was out there paddling and having the time of my life. Absolutely fantastic.

But in August, I left the canoe, summer, and school behind. My father sent me to Simmonds of Tonbridge to apprentice as a tailor. I went to this shop to learn what was expected of me, and from the start, I felt like a trapped bird.

These were older gentlemen who worked there, some ex-military, the type of people who have served. The highlight of my day was when they sent me up to the stock room to go and find something. I jumped to it, "All right, I'll get it down there in two seconds." That was fun. Everything else was . . .

I worked, and had a room at a boarding house there, but I wasn't getting paid anything. They were all nice people, but I struggled with it. I had this vision . . . I could see myself being on an airplane in Egypt. I could see myself, much like the movies, being elsewhere.

On the weekends, I used to go up to Manston Airport and Invicta

International's operations building. I'd walk in there and just have a look around, and I used to talk backwards and forwards with Steve, the operations manager for Invicta.

An old World War II Nissan hut building served as the operation center. Out in front was a big concrete ramp, with grass and the main runway up to the left. All the airplanes would come in there to taxi to a stop, and they used to push them back with their nose facing outwards toward operations, all the way down the ramp.

The operations office was expansive, with giant windows that looked over the whole airfield. The ramp was in front of you. A large desk ran along the wall and wrapped around the corner. The crews used to come in directly from their flights or to get their briefing. A telex was a vital piece of equipment.

Everything was interesting to me. The technology. The smell. The stories and information. Where the pilots were going, what interesting people they met, where they were taking people, who were they going to see. How does all this get put together? How do they make money? How does the fuel get in these things? All of that stuff.

I traveled the tight circle between my apprenticeship and my home until one weekend. I happened to go by Invicta's operations office, and I was just about to ask, "What's the possibility of ever getting a job here?"

But before I was able to get the words out, Steve said, "You know, we're actually looking for somebody as an Ops Clerk. Would you like a job?"

On my way back to Tonbridge, I was walking on a cloud.

As a side note, I have high hopes for the future of Manston. In fact, after being closed recently, the airport has just been given permission to reopen again. Through the work of many other people and myself at the Save Manston Association, the airport will hopefully come back to life soon.

I have a vision that Manston will become an important hub fifty years on from now. By that stage, cars will be autonomous, as well as buses, ambulances, trains, and airplanes. And so, there will be no airport parking. No need for any shops. You will just turn up, get on board, and go.

But airports will still be needed in the future. No question.

Currently, all three London airports are so chock-a-block that they consequently raise passenger fares because there's nowhere to land. Then they've got all these cargo airplanes. Cargo is a monster nowadays with Amazon and things like that.

I see Manston as a diamond in the rough. I believe you've got to look fifty years ahead. Not twenty-five, but fifty years. Otherwise, you will run out of space.

Because what so often happens with airports is that two or three years after one is built, everyone decides it's not big enough. So, they renovate the airport again, causing all amount of trouble and congestion.

Long-term planning must be considered. I call it "Full Circle" because of my love of aviation, what it gave me, and my respect for the people I met and worked with there.

Tailor-Made to Fly

CHAPTER 2

On Your Mark

"You start with a bag full of luck and an empty bag of experience. The trick is to fill the bag of experience before you empty the bag of luck." — Unknown

W HEN I STARTED AT Invicta International as an operations clerk, I was sixteen years old.

An important part of my job at Invicta was to post the NOTAMs (notice to airmen) on the briefing board every day. I used to speak to the crews, bring them to be briefed by the Royal Airforce Duty Officer, and drive flight crews to the tower. NOTAMs were sent out daily by the Civil Aviation Authority (CAA) in London and sent by Royal Mail.

If you were flying to Milan or Cairo or down into Nairobi, these NOTAMs would tell the pilot what to expect when landing at their destination, whether any work was being performed on the runway, and where to park. It was the best way to eliminate or minimize problems. The NOTAMs were kind of like a trip map.

So, my job was to put these NOTAM up every single day on clipboards arranged by country and continent on a large wall within the operations building. Then, when crews came in, it was also my job to run them around, take them to the airplane, and alert maintenance to call and put the ground power unit on.

I would also post information on the wall in the operations center, where the airplanes were going, their routes, and flight numbers. I was promoted from clerk to a duty officer in no time at all. When an airplane flies to foreign countries, it's necessary to apply for a clearance to fly over each country on the way to the final destination. I had to apply for these permits to get our airplanes over foreign countries. I also had to apply in advance for overflight, traffic landing rights, and handling when the aircraft landed.

On an aviation map, that is called the Flight Information Region, or FIR boundary, and that means the physical boundary of each country, and up to 250 miles out if you're over water. In each clearance application, you have to record the time you enter, how long you're going to be there, and what time you leave. Any official who reviews the airspace can look up your flight number and know about that airplane, where it's coming from, and where it's going.

For example, you take off from the airport, and you fly over France. You would have to apply in France, apply to Italy, and apply to each country. If you're going down to Africa, that's a lot of applying. They would send back a code, and that's the code they would look for. But if they didn't see it, they would radio and confirm the code before the aircraft was permitted to proceed.

And so, I got the permits for our planes. Otherwise, they couldn't get the crews picked up, and they couldn't get fuel, all the essentials an airplane needs. If the receiving airport didn't know their plans, they didn't get anything. And they also had to obtain permission to land at the airport and to make sure there was a stand for them.

It was tremendous groundwork for me, and I had the opportunity to learn a vast amount. It was almost like opening up an encyclopedia and saying, "Okay, what do you want to learn next?" Unless you're really in the trenches and doing the work yourself, it's tough to get that knowledge that's so vital. The basics like flight, speaking to people, communications, and customer service. If you don't put down the sand and then the concrete, the foundation is never grounded.

Because Manston was still a Royal Air Force working military base, one side was military, and the other was civilian. The military was used to having the crews go over to the tower, all the way up to the tower, and then report to a Royal Air Force Officer who briefed them as to what to look for going.

I remember thinking, "That's crazy. The same crew taxis in. Nothing has changed, and now they are taxiing out. Why do they need to see them? It doesn't make sense." Of course, it didn't, but that was just the way it was.

I just had so much fun there. I used to operate the radio. The airplanes would call in when they were maybe forty-five minutes out, "IM754 Manston inbound to you, estimating arrival . . ." And then I would say, "Roger," and call up maintenance to alert them that the planes were on their way in. Maintenance would bring out the tow bar, aircraft passenger stairs, ground power unit, and have all the equipment ready to service the airplane.

Some days, I would write and fill the giant operations board that used to stretch across the entire back wall. It had everything: which airplanes were coming in from here, arriving from there, leaving again, so everybody knew what was going on.

A lot of cargo moved out of Manston to foreign destinations, since European goods were very much in demand. In Africa, they didn't have refrigerators. Or tooling. Everything came out of Europe to go down to Africa and wherever. During those days, Africa was a big buyer destination. All the way down through Africa, then to India and Asia. Not like it is now. All the modern products were manufactured in Europe. On the return flight, the airplane was full of fruit and vegetables, whatever we could possibly take as a back load to help pay for the return fuel. The airlines made their money in the outbound, not the inbound. If you could bring back something of value, that was excellent. Back then, coffee wasn't even on the map.

About this same time, I also began flying lessons with Kelvin Sheen, who became a good friend at the Kent Flying Club. I went up with him on a flying lesson one day. He took the Cessna 150 up and asked me if I wanted to fly it. And I said, "Absolutely! Let me have a go!" From there, I got the bug and decided to get my pilot's wings. That was where I learned to fly.

Manston was used as a base for bringing Volkswagen and Audi parts in from Germany. Ted Cooper piloted the brand-new Cessna 404 Titan to pick up the parts. The plane was a single pilot operation, and he didn't need a co-pilot. But on my days off from working at Invicta, or anytime I could, I was on the airplane with Ted. He put me in the seat, and I became a safety pilot for him. Our association lasted during my time at Invicta, then when I was with IAS Cargo Airlines, and all the way to when I was in Luton. A long time.

Even when the airplane moved from Luton to Cranfield, I met him up in Cranfield.

The airplane used to fly empty to Germany then return with the parts, back and forth, so I was able to build up my hours. I learned such a lot through him. Such a wonderful gentleman. He had a mustache and used to smoke like a trooper. But he would come into the operations hut in the morning to get his briefing, come around and talk, have a cup of coffee, and then we used to fly off. He had this big sheep's wool jacket, like something the early RAF pilots used to wear because it was so cold in the airplane. The old aircraft, but not the newer plane. The new plane was lovely. But he was a character, and I salute him. He taught me a great deal.

And for me, my mother used to know when to put dinner on because she could hear the airplane coming over the rooftop on our way back from Germany.

While working at Invicta and flying with Ted, I got my first taste of charter service. Occasionally, we did more than fly parts. We also flew VW company executives. One particular time, we took some English executives out to this place in Denmark. It was on the water, quite the resort. I was invited into a boardroom with them as they were doing a presentation. We had dinner together and went out at night. I was young, but the impression it made was like, holy moly. This was how executives were looked after in Denmark! It was an eye-opener!

The Danish company we visited manufactured big garage-sized

plastic signs like the ones you see at gas stations, Chevron and Esso and BP. They were putting in a bid to Volkswagen, who was changing their logo at the time. They became the company that re-did all of Volkswagen's signs, the ones you still see today, all designed and developed by this company in Denmark.

I remember sitting at the conference table and thinking that this was all possible because of our airplane. The meeting was a graphic example of what the aircraft could accomplish, transporting the executives so they could get their job done.

Back at the airport, the weather was beautiful that afternoon and into the evening at the Volkswagen base. But when we called up the weather forecast for our return destination, we were told that the whole of the southeast of England was fogged in. We took off anyway, and as we got closer and closer to London, we could hear people on the radio chattering about going left, right, and center to avoid the fog. But luck was with us. We ended up being the very last airplane to get into our base at Manston.

We were the only airplane to get into Manston that night.

Everybody was trying to get in behind us, but nobody could fly in. As we were landing on the runway, the fog was coming up fast. After we landed with all the executives on board, a "follow me" vehicle from the airport came out to find us, so we could make our way back into the ramp. That was how bad the fog was.

One day when flying for Volkswagen, Ted and I had to deal with a bomb scare. This was around 1977 when the IRA in England was a big issue. There were some terrible bombings in Northern Ireland and the pubs in England. Really sad. We used to hear about it in London, which was only an hour and a half away.

I remember that it was a beautiful sunny day in the early spring. Down at the Nissen Hut, where our operations office was located, there was a little door. I opened the red door, went down three steps, and the airplane was parked right there. Still a slight chill in the air, I walked out to the airplane on the ramp.

As was our habit, Ted went to file the flight plan, and I did the walk around and removed the tie-down of the airplane. The morning dew was still on the aircraft, and I could feel the warmth of the air coming up through the chill.

Checking the oil, I made sure all was as it should be. All the airplane mechanics, the elevator aileron, and the rudders were all free and clear. I made sure no birds had made any nests in there overnight.

Ted and I got in the airplane, like we usually did, and started the engines up. I had a coffee flask right next to me, and Ted had one as well. We got the clearance from the tower and taxied out to the end runway; then, we performed the engine run-ups. Just to make sure everything was good. Then, finally, we got airborne out of Manston.

We took off on runway 11 as it was the one that went inland, made the turnout, and headed towards Dover. We were probably up to 7,000 to 8,000 feet and had just gotten to the point where the air traffic controllers handed us over to France.

While we were speaking to France, they said, "Golf Victor Whisky Golf Bravo. We've just received a phone call from Manston Military. Can you please go back on frequency?"

We changed over to frequency and Kent Radar, controlled within the RAF Manston tower, transmitted, "Golf Victor Whisky Golf Bravo. We've just had a strange call to say that your aircraft might have a possible explosive device on board."

"What?" Ted looked at me, and I looked at Ted.

I said, "I did the walk around. I looked in the engine bay, and I didn't see anything."

Ted replied, "We acknowledge. Standby."

We elected to take up a hold in the middle of the English Channel. We did that…

And then we debated. We thought about it and considered all our options. Where could we go? "Well, if it's a hoax, but what if it's not . . ."

The nearest place to land was Liège, across the Channel in Belgium.

We could go in there, but if there was an issue, we could be stuck there for a long time.

Then Ted, obviously the one with the brains, said, "Stupid! We'll just go back to Manston. It's military. They'll have everything we need there."

We called Manston and said, "We're going to come back to you. We'd like to descend to water level because if something does happen, we'll end up in the English Channel pretty quickly."

And that was what we did.

We were flying down so low and close to the water level that the props kicked up spray behind the airplane.

We zipped past a Ramsgate-to-Calais passenger hovercraft on its return journey to Ramsgate. We were probably at about the same height as the top of the hovercraft, and the passengers must have been gawking and puzzled about what was going on!

As we landed at Manston, all the fire trucks followed us down the runway. Because Manston was a military airport, they had these lots of dispersal areas where airplanes used to be positioned during the Second World War. Each site was quite a way apart from each other and dotted at various concrete pads all over the place. So, in the advent of an attack, the enemy may be able to blow up one airplane, but they couldn't destroy all of them.

We were directed to stop at one of these pads, right smack in the middle of the airport.

Ted shut the engines down, told me to get out, and then came after me. We stood away from the airplane, discussed possibilities, and waited until they sent down a bomb dog from Maidstone, about two hours away. We eventually went back to the airport operations office, and had a cup of coffee, and then came back when the inspector with the bomb dog turned up.

But before inspecting the airplane, the dog took a restroom stop. Later, as the handler walked around the aircraft, the unlucky man stepped in the dog's poo, slipped, and landed right on his butt.

That was the only laugh of the day.

The inspector didn't find anything, so we fueled up, and off we went back to Germany.

I didn't feel frightened or anything. I was confident that I had done a proper look around, and I didn't see anything. But there was always that nagging question . . . Was the threat real?

The only possibility we could possibly think of was that there might have been a pressure switch.

I had looked in and around the wheels, but I didn't look into the space where the wheels retract during flight. As the wheels come up, there could have been a pressure switch above the wheels that might have been hit. I thought that I probably would have noticed it, but I had to ask myself: What if I didn't?

But that was me being pretty technical as well as philosophical. Back then, these were nasty bombs made of bangs and nuts and bolts and stuff. Nothing James Bond-ish at all.

Later in my career, I worked for EL AL Israeli Airlines and learned a great deal about the safety and security protocols that I so often use in my career today. Whenever an EL AL airplane lands in the world, it is 100% safe. Wherever it lands, the aircraft is on constant visual. A guard does not leave that airplane until it takes off again.

There are so many checks and protocols.

In the event of an issue, they can put the suspected package in a particular place on the airplane, so if it did happen to detonate, there would not be a problem. The operation is that tight.

We used to take the Volkswagen and Audi parts all over Scandinavia, France, United Kingdom, Jersey, the Channel Islands. That was what Ted, and the airplane were used for. But our main route was to go back and forth from Manston to Germany to supply the factory in Ramsgate.

I do love flying. When you are up in the skies, in the evening, or the morning, there's nothing like it. It's serene, tranquil. All you have are the sound of the engines, and looking down, you see the blues and pinks, the golds and greens. It's the best view you can see. It's magical. I can only imagine that with astronauts in space, that incredible view would be magnified. You have a sense of freedom, almost like a bird.

I think most pilots — maybe even every single pilot who is in it for a career — are not in the business for the job. I think aviation professionals have a passion for flying. While they mumble about the pay, I think the core of being a pilot and of working in aviation and aerospace is the passion. At times, things can be problematic with passengers, with the business and the system it's created, but at the essence of it all, I feel most pilots would agree with me that it's an honor to do what we do.

Whether I realized it or not at the time, the most valuable lessons I've learned and the foundation for what I do today were already starting to assert themselves. My operating principles went back to my father's business, even though I didn't recognize and connect the two at the time. My father was very good with all the customers. I used to see him speak to the customers. He was very respectful of what they wanted, and he listened to them.

That's management lesson number one: Listen to the customer.

And the second essential management lesson?

Timeliness. Time is the most important commodity on the planet for us as human beings. But, unfortunately, it's the most important when it comes to life matters; we don't have much time.

It's very disrespectful if you don't arrive on time, or if you don't depart on time. It affects everybody's lives, your guests, your customers, whoever, or if you're moving freight. There used to be an old analogy, passengers need to go on time, but it doesn't matter if freight is on time.

People used to say the good thing about flying cargo is that it doesn't talk back to you.

However, this was before Federal Express, and all the other companies like them. Freight does complain nowadays!

My main job at Invicta was in operations as an operations clerk, and I absolutely loved it. I learned how to write out my own passenger tickets, Manston to Milan. For insurance purposes and legally, you have to have a ticket.

And I would fly any chance I could get. I would go on the flights as a supernumerary crew member. I was not a member of the crew; I had nothing to do with the crew. I was just on board lapping up the experience, seeing and learning what they do. Sometimes, because they knew I was getting my license, they used to let me fly the airplane.

Manston — well, really, England itself — is famous for two types of weather conditions: wind and fog.

First, wind. When you're out in the winter winds in England, you're walking at an angle. You can imagine that landing at Manston in a crosswind was quite the adventure.

Many of the pilots and co-pilots at the time were old, either in their retirement years or just coming into them. But they were all extremely experienced, very much a man in the machine working with the elements.

The Britannia was a beautiful, luxury airplane, but it was a monster to fly. You needed really sophisticated people to fly this machine and be able to put it on the ground. You needed the best totality of the crew's ability, the captain, the co-pilot, the flight engineer to make that happen.

I remember one time when it was icy on the runway. There was also a lot of wind and rain. On that particular return flight, we were very close to the airplane's maximum crosswind performance. There was a real question whether we could get in or not.

I was actually standing behind the crew, watching them as they were landing the plane. I was still in my teens, and I can still see the guys and hear them saying, "You have control!" and "Okay, I've got control!" They had to work together, fighting aggressively to get the airplane down when it was up against its limits in severe wind and ice conditions.

When we touched down, the airplane was wagging its tail. Not out of control, but maybe a controlled out of control. The captain wrestled with that bucking bronco, like a huge ape on drugs, trying to put the plane on the ground and keep it from going off the runway. The pilots of that era weren't daredevils; they were true professionals.

The mechanics of the aircraft at that time were all cable. Whether you pulled the stick back, turned right, or turned left, it was cables going all the way to the elevators and the ailerons and tail that made the airplane fly. Hence, operating the controls was a very physical endeavor, and that was why that captain looked like a gorilla, flying an airplane simply because he had to work at it.

Although the Britannia was an airplane that was all cable-driven, the instrument panels and navigation system were electric, a brand-new innovation when it was built. But electricity could cause other complications when we had animals as cargo. For example, we used to take calves to Venice and Milan quite a lot because Italy is known for liking its veal. We would fly a cargo of calves on board, 3 or 4 times a week, from Manston to Venice or Milan, then turn around and fly back.

When the calves were loaded in the back, they would go up the ramp into metal pens that looked like scaffolding. We used to put twenty-five in each pen, close it up with two additional pieces of scaffolding and place hay on the floor.

As soon as one group finished loading, we would close that pen, then repeat the process until the calves were on board all the way to the front.

During the winter months, the airplane looked like it was on fire, but it wasn't. The animals were so warm that their breath would turn into condensation. When the freight door was open and, illuminated by the night ramp lights coming down from the airport, all this moisture would billow from the inside of the cargo hold and look like smoke. But the apparent smoke was simply the concentrated moisture from the calves' breath. We didn't actually need temperature control in the back of the airplane because the calves would warm it up. They produced their own climate. The best way to explain it would be for you to picture walking into your house right now, but with lots of calves visiting. They would pump the humidity up so much; it would be as if your house just turned into Hawaii.

We would take off out of Manston, cross over Dover, and get up to altitude over France, about 21,000 to 32,000 feet, and then as we climbed to a higher altitude, over the top of the Italian Alps, we would run into problems.

As I said, the Bristol Britannia was all-electric, one of the very first airplanes that was all-electric, but guess what? You had the calves in the back of the airplane. And what do calves do? Their breath produces tons of humidity. The amount of moisture they generate is astronomic, truly unbelievable.

As we climbed higher to get over the Alps, the outside of the aircraft got cold, then the entire inside of the airplane became cold, cold-soaked. The moisture from the calves, as soon as it stuck to the cold surface of the inside of the plane froze, including the windows.

Behind the cockpit doors were located all the circuit breakers, down the left-hand side of the airplane behind the captain and also behind the flight engineer's panel. These were the circuits, and of course, they were little buttons. If a circuit blew, these little buttons used to pop out. Everything in the cockpit would freeze up, all the buttons and everything else.

On the descent, the flight engineer would get up and position his seat to prepare. Then he placed his feet, one underneath the flight engineer's seat and another one under the captain's seat, in anticipation of the thawing moisture from the frozen humidity that would trickle down behind the circuit breakers in the instrument panel.

As we descended from the high altitude into the warmer air of the Mediterranean, all of a sudden, as we were flying, "Bing," the radio button would pop off or one of the navigation systems buttons. The flight engineer had to keep a watchful eye, looking around and going, "Oh, that's that circuit breaker that popped." He would reset the button to get the instrument back online. He would have to be pushing buttons in to reconnect the electrical equipment just to keep the airplane flying!

And this all happened because of the calves!

On other occasions, after passing through the turbulence of getting airborne, I would open the cockpit door and see a calf coming toward me.

I was like, "How did you get out of your pen? Get back in there." But the calf would just stand there licking the door handle. Their tongues licked everything. All of those things were fun, tremendously fun experiences.

The second weather mainstay in England is our famous fog. Back at my regular job in operations at Manston, I learned about diversions because of all the airplanes coming in from different companies, such as British Airways,

One evening, I was working, and after the sun went down, the fog started rolling in. Sometimes, very rarely, we used to get diversions to Manston when the weather made it difficult to land at other airports. If we did get any, it would most often happen in the fall. We shared the same radio frequency with quite a few airlines going into London, Gatwick, serviced by Airlines such as British Caledonian and Dan Air in addition to other airlines using the same radio frequency as far away as London-Luton, based airlines included Monarch Airlines and Britannia Airways.

But this particular evening, all these airplanes were coming up, all the way from Africa, Larnaca, Frankfurt, all over the place. They were coming in, and they were speaking to company operation. I could hear them going around from one to the other, saying, "Where would you like us to go?"

They were all searching for a place to land.

So, I made a command decision. I didn't ask anyone's permission.

Later, my co-workers told me I was shaking, that I was positively shaking with excitement, but I don't really know if it was excitement or nervousness. I do remember thinking, "This is ridiculous. All these planes are going back. They're turning around. They're going back to where they came from, back to Europe. That's ridiculous."

And other airplanes were still coming.

I thought, "They can't do that."

I remember this one Caledonian flight coming inbound, and I said to myself, "Okay, I'm doing it."

I picked up the company radio and said, "Caledonian 7-5, (or whatever it was). This is Manston. Just to let you know, we're clear. CAVOK. No weather problems."

Whoever was on the radio immediately answered me back. I heard them speaking to their operations, asking, "Can we go to . . . What's Manston? Can we use Manston?"

Then the phone rang.

I picked it up, and a voice on the other end said, "Can you handle the airplane?"

I replied, "Yeah, sure." Then as I put down the phone, I thought, "Oh shit! I haven't called anybody!"

I made some calls. I called down to Red, this maintenance hangar guy, a very nice person, an American who married a British girl after the war. I was afraid he was probably going to lie to me, but I called up and asked, "Hey, can we handle an airplane, a couple of airplanes. You know, one airplane. Whatever."

And he said, "Sure, why not? I'll bring the tug down."

Then I thought, "Crap. I've got no customs."

But I did know a customs guy who used to take photographs of airplanes. I still have some of his photographs. He loved airplanes. I knew I could get him on my side, so I called him up and said, "Would you mind handling a couple of airplanes?"

He said, "Sure, how many?"

I said, "I don't know."

But he still said, "Sure."

I called them back and said, "Yep. No problem at all. We can handle all that."

The first plane to land was a 707. Back then, that was a large airplane. As soon as I confirmed that we could accommodate that Caledonian flight on the radio, all these other airplanes that were in holding patterns searching for places to land started chattering, "Manston? Where's Manston?"

Manston is forty minutes away from Gatwick. Absolutely, it was the right place to go.

Suddenly, I had six or seven airplanes calling up. I'm like, "Holy shit!" All these airplanes started to land. We actually had a big ramp because it was built as a military ramp.

The next problem I had was buses. I needed buses. I called up the buses guy who inquired, "How many buses do you need?"

I said, "A hundred and seventy-five passengers per airplane. Nine buses. For now!"

"Haven't got that many."

"Can you go get them?"

"Yes."

It was a lovely night, and I worked there until three o'clock in the morning. Eventually, Manston got fogged in as well, somewhere around eleven o'clock that night, so we couldn't accept any more airplanes.

I went home and went to bed. I didn't call my boss. I didn't tell anybody that this was happening. It just happened. I didn't think about it.

The next morning as I rounded the corner on my way to the airport, there were all these tails of 707s, BAC1-11s, Handley Page Dart Heralds sitting there, parked and waiting.

You did not normally see stuff like this at Manston.

When I walked into the office, everyone stood looking at me, and said, "Okay. What happened?"

Then Hugh Kennard himself came up to me, and he shook my hand. He said, "You're going to be something in aviation."

Now, as I look over my aviation career, when somebody tells me it can't be done, I say, "Why not? We used to do that, and this is the way we got around it, and this is the way we did it." I think if you consider the present day, a lot of people have forgotten how things were done.

I have flown into Nigeria quite a few times in the past, and you didn't have a cell phone, you didn't have a radio, you didn't have anything. The only way to communicate was to get into the cockpit and dial into the HF high-frequency radio. I'd call up on the radio, find someone in operations at the airport where we would be landing, and ask them to go and find workers to unload the cargo. You know, that was why we always carried a crate of whiskey in the back. Usually, the reply I got was, "Sure, no problem, be over there when you land."

CHAPTER 3

The Big Time

*"When once you have tasted flight, you will forever walk the
earth with your eyes turned skyward, for there you have been,
and there you will always long to return."*
— Leonardo DaVinci

W HEN I WORKED AT Invicta, we would fill the planes with
cargo, freight, and animals, readying them to fly all over the
world. I watched the airplanes startup, get to the end of the runway,
and be off. I used to think, "Where are they going to? What adventures
will they have?"

Just like when I was a boy.

For me, that was a pull, and I knew I had to go on, advance to the
next step.

Invicta was great. I handled all these airplanes coming and going.
Fantastic. But after a couple of years, I felt that I was ready for more.
I wanted to spread my wings, to go and see more of the world. I
wanted to work at the big city airport. I wanted to see the big stuff. I
had a draw, a yearning.

When a job came available, I started as an operations assistant at
IAS Cargo Airlines based out of London Gatwick. I left Invicta to
work for IAS because of bright lights, big airplanes, and that
wanderlust of adventure.

I was eighteen at the time.

In 1978, IAS Cargo was one of the UK's more prominent cargo airlines. They would fly DC-8s around the world, literally. They used to get nineteen hours a day out of the airplanes, which was unbelievable.

Part of my job at IAS operations Gatwick was to take the DC-8 flight crews out to the ramp, brief the crews, and make sure everything else was ready to go so the airplane could depart.

My shifts were four days on, four days off. I used to work two days, then two nights — four days on, four days off. When I came on duty, I would see a DC-8 out on that very first day. By the time I was about to go off duty, that airplane would have traveled around the world.

That was the attraction, the lure.

I went to work for IAS Cargo Airlines to gain this experience. A complete cargo change without changing the crew, used to take an hour which is pretty quick. If a crew change was added to the cargo change, then we slotted an hour and a half.

From Gatwick, the plane would go to all these places in Africa; then from Africa over the Indian Ocean down to Australia; then across the Pacific to America; and then back to the United Kingdom. The experience was remarkable.

I can still remember all the ramps and the Caledonia DC-10s parked up against the gate and the pretty Laker airplanes. All these trucks were going everywhere.

I was like, "Okay, I'm happy."

IAS was very efficient. The company had eight DC-8s. As I mentioned, we used to get around the world in roughly four days. Fantastic. It was state of the art, brilliant. So, every night we used to have this thing called the May Fly.

The May Fly was a list of everything happening, including the tail number of the aircraft, where it was going, the freight load, and how many crew members were on board. Every single night, one of the duty officers from Hawley had to drive this list around to every single place.

There wasn't any kind of faxing or texting back then, so we had to physically deliver the list to everyone who had to have it.

We went to the caterers first so they would know the departure time of the airplane and be able to prepare and bring the crew meals onboard for the aircraft. Next, we took it to the handling agents, who needed to know what time the cargo would arrive in the warehouse. They also had to know what time the pallet was being built to go on the airplanes that were flying out the next day. Then, finally, we had to drive it to the fueling people. We would take the list to each consecutive department, about nine different stops, all the way around London Gatwick. That job alone used to take about forty-five minutes every day.

But that meant that the next day went squeaky clean.

Everything was on time because of the May Fly.

During my early tenure with Alpha Jet, and even with Le Bas International, I basically developed the same type of May Fly list of airplanes available for our clients. Most of them are airline class. I used the same concept: I listed available planes, their location, and how long the call out. We had twelve fax lines, and every night, I automatically sent out faxes to all our clients so they would know where the airplanes were. Everybody does this now, but at that time, we were ahead of the curve. But this list at IAS Cargo was where I first encountered the original May Fly. That was how it all came about.

For Le Bas International, I turned the original idea around and gave it to our clients. Then they could now see, "Oh, they've got availability there, they've got it here." In the back of our customer's mind, we've built our reputation, and they trust that when they need a flight, they know right where they can go.

Also, it's beneficial for our business because the client immediately knows what aircraft are available and where they stand. "Le Bas, hold it — they have it right there. Call them now. They've got an airplane ready. They've got a crew. Hang on — they've got a crew time of forty-five minutes. Hang on. We need that, that there. Yup that will work. That will help us out, recover this airplane. We need them. Call them."

You get the picture.

IAS Cargo used the May Fly list to communicate with everybody efficiently, and everybody looked at that. They used to put it up on the clipboard. I've still got the clipboard with stickers of so many airlines on the back of it, all the companies covered by the May Fly. The duty officer used to put the information on the clipboard. When people came on shift in the morning, they would look at it and say, "Okay, I've got to be there first, then there, got to be there."

Our operations room was very large then. Around the corner, there was the manager's room where the crewing people gathered. We had then, and I still use it today, this longboard that projected two weeks ahead, where we wrote all the airplanes' comings and goings.

The registrations were on the left-hand side. Then there was a long line going all the way out telling what the airplanes were doing, the flight numbers, and the time they were scheduled to leave. The board would be updated on take-off. You would put a line through the scheduled time and rub it out, then put the actual time departure in a different color, the ETA (estimated time of arrival), and what load was in the airplane.

At that time, we had a TV screen facing that board, which was state of the art. Upstairs was the commercial department where they booked flights, and they had the same similar TV screen. It was an excellent system where we could see what they were updating on the screen. As they updated it upstairs in the commercial department, the information was also available on the screen below.

I used a similar setup until only a couple of years ago. The twenty-four-hour clock was in use, so one block was twenty-four hours. The information put on the board was the flight number, departure, London Gatwick, LGW, going into Dubai, DXB. Flight number and the captain's name was underneath, along with how much freight was on board, and the fuel requirements.

In the crew department, they had the same thing. That was how they would schedule crews to get into the airplane because we were on turnarounds every hour and a half. When will the crews get there? Do they have enough duty? How long are they going to be, i.e., the duty time? Can we make that hour and a half turn? The whole operation could be pretty mind-boggling, but I had to learn the system.

And then we had Telexes right next door to operations. We had eight different Telexes, with workers in there twenty-four hours a day. It's called SITA, and it's still around. Founded in 1949, the Air Transport Communications and Information Technology headquarters is in Geneva, Switzerland. So, for instance, London Gatwick, for our office, would be LGWOOFF with the OO meaning operations and Fox Fox is the airline code for IAS. So, if I were to send it to British Airways in Athens, it would be ATHOOBA as an example.

We would then write a note out and put it through the slot in the window. The office personnel typed out this message. So, for example, the message could be sent anywhere in the world such as stations in Melbourne or Sidney (SYD), Australia, to our handling agent, where our station manager retrieved the information straight away as soon as it was QU, a priority code within the SITA language. So as soon as we hit it, there was a message going. And he would say, "Okay, it's off, it's airborne." And then the station manager or handling agents notified all the people needed to service the airplane. That was how we performed the turnaround so quickly. Fascinating. To me at the time, it was like, "Oh my God."

Now, we track airplanes. When our customer has a flight with us, we know the aircraft's tail number and the vendor we're using. They share that with us, and as soon as we know, we send the link to the customer to share if they want to. If they have a secretary, they can send it on to their secretary to track. If they have family, they can share it with their family member. They have a code that allows them to access the information about the flight. Once they have the code, if they're sitting in the airplane, they can see themselves going through the skies like Flight Tracker. But we always send our customers the information for their aircraft.

These details are crucial when it comes to maintaining client privacy . . . Private is private. We send it out with a reference number, and that reference number changes for every flight for security reasons. Once that particular reference number is used, it's gone. We only use a specific reference number one time.

If this system goes down, we do have backup generators. But again, we are always prepared to go back to basics. If need be, we can still speak directly to the tower. We can still get a message out or receive a notification. So, the Air Traffic Control (ATC) system still exists, though it's now called Aeronautical Fixed Telecommunications Network (AFTN). When an airplane departs with a filed flight plan, this sends a message AFTN to each one of the stations — control tower or presence — that follows the flight along the way to the final destination.

That system built way back when is still around. If all else fails, it's there. In the event of an incident, or even if an aircraft is overdue for thirty minutes, then an automatic warning goes out.

"Where is the airplane?"

Despite having a backup, and a backup to the backup, things go wrong all the time with planes and air travel. One of the things I enjoy most about my job is that we get to assist other aviators. Le Bas International currently offers our airline services program. Over my career, it has been an honour and a privilege to support over 187 airlines around the globe. In addition to that, we service 95% of the globe's aircraft manufacturers' private flight departments and Maintenance Repair and Overhaul (MROs). When their airplane has a technical problem, and they need supplementary uplift, we help them.

But we also support what's known as Go Teams.

Most airlines, in their operations center, have a special area set aside in the event of an incident. It's a room that has everything needed in an emergency. Those airlines have "emergency training" sessions in which specific team members are trained to depart the operations center and go into this facility. They have state of the art communications in there. Our Go Teams become part of that emergency team, which often consists of the airline's chief pilot; the director of maintenance; customer care people; and other specialists.

As part of our Aerospace services, we offer airplanes dotted throughout the globe for these airlines, in the event of a situation or issue. It's unfortunate, but you need people ready to help. We offer airplanes that can go on a moment's notice to take them to the destination so they can do what needs to be done. The mission is to move the operation in a positive environment, no matter the circumstance.

In the office next to the IAS Cargo operations center, we had eight telexes in a line along with telex operators. The commercial side of operations used to send out form messages that were so effective that when people received the notes, they would immediately understand the information.

I learned that whenever a station manager anywhere in the world — Lagos, Australia, South Africa, or New York, would get this message, he could understand it straight away without going into detail.

We also used Berna Radio, a high-frequency (HF) radio, still used today, which operates like an open mic. You can relay information short and abrupt to your company using this. However, everybody uses that frequency if you are in the area. You might be on the same frequency as British Airways or on the same frequency as Air Afrique. Or South African Airways or Saudi Arabian Airlines.

Depending on where you are flying in the world, you turn to different frequencies to use Berna Radio, and you have a call sign. For example, Hotel Bravo Echo Mike Charlie was one of our call signs. Airlines had an account with Berna Radio, and each aircraft had a call sign with Berna Radio.

When the aircraft departed, the crew used to call up and say, "Berna Radio, Berna Radio, this is Fox Fox 285," which was the flight number. Their response would be, "Fox Fox 285, go ahead." The flight crew would go on, "Fox Fox 285, we're airborne out of LFPG at 2345." Then the crew would give the load, "Load of," whatever the cargo was. Let's say, "32,500 kilos and fuel onboard, ETA Johannesburg, JNB at 0542." Then they would sign off.

At that point, I would take the message, go to the operations board, and write that up. Then that same message would be taken to the telex room and sent down to Johannesburg. The station manager would have all the information they needed.

More detailed information was probably given on what was on board, where it was, and everything like that. When the airplane landed, everyone knew what cargo was on board and where the payload had to go. It was so well-organized.

Now, on each airplane, cell phones are widely used. You can make cell phone calls on airplanes, no problem today. That's how most planes currently communicate. But then, on an HF radio, each aircraft had a cell call code. Depending on what hemisphere you were in the world, you would use specific frequencies.

While I worked at IAS, I was also part of IAS Courier Services, which transported mail in the early days of air transport before Federal Express. I used to take company mail and corporate mail. If you wanted to expedite written communication to Africa or anywhere else, you had to hire a special service. Regular post used to take two to three weeks, maybe up to a month. For speed and security, our courier service was in high demand.

IAS maintained twelve offices all over the world. One of the offices that I used to go to quite a lot was in Lagos, Nigeria.

Different companies would bring their mail or parcels to Gatwick in the morning, and by the following day, the item would be in Nigeria, Kinshasa, or Johannesburg. Travel time was speedy. Quicker than it is nowadays, believe it or not. I remember receiving the mail, putting it in a big pouch, then hopping on a British Caledonian flight to Africa.

The company used to position us around, so someone would be available to take a job at all times. Since I was working operations, I used to go on company flights down — IAS airplanes — to the station where I needed to drop the mail. I did this on my days off as well because I would get extra pay.

I thought it was great. Going in an airplane to Africa, why wouldn't you do that? Hello!

On my first time going into Nigeria specifically, I felt like I was in a candy store filled with untold delights. "What sweet do I try next?" This was a completely different experience.

I had a visa, and I got all recommended immunizations for where I would be going. I got shots against typhoid, cholera, yellow fever, all that stuff. And then I would also have to get entry stamps from individual countries. So now and again, the company would take our passports from embassy to embassy to collect the entry stamps.

At that time, the airplanes used to frequently fly down because there were a lot of things opening up in Africa. Significant investments and everything were moving by air.

Other times when I flew down there, I would take a commercial British Caledonian flight. They were a terrific airline, absolutely fantastic. Professional to the T. If anybody could experience what they did then, their jaws would drop.

I was a total workaholic.

Sometimes I would stay up in Gatwick after work. But intermittently, I used to go home after doing courier flights to various places in Africa.

I would get home and just get into bed, then the phone would ring, and it would be IAS. They said, "Such and such can't do the flight tonight going to wherever it was in Africa. Can you do it?" I answered, "Yep, absolutely." I just got home and had a meal, only to get back in the airplane again to go off to Africa.

Africa is such a different place. On our flights, I used to get in the DC-8 and sit in the jump seat going down. I can still see the DC-8 departing. We usually used to depart in the evening out of Gatwick. On the flight down, I would sit and watch the pilots do their stuff. I thought it was all fascinating.

Sometimes I would travel to Lagos, which used to be the capital of

Nigeria. Abuja is the current capital of Nigeria, located in the central part of Nigeria, in Federal Capital Territory. The city is approximately 300 miles (480 km) northeast of Lagos, the former capital.

It was such a completely different world than what I was used to. Sometimes we'd fly over the top of Lagos about 4:00, 4:45 in the morning. The dawn would be coming up, and the pilot would call up the tower. When you were going over England and Europe, you spoke to everybody. But then when you departed Spain and got over Africa, there was nobody there. Nothing.

The only way you speak to other airplanes was by HF radio. You got on the radio wherever you were. You're on a frequency, an actual radio frequency. The crews would just tell you what altitude to be at and the plane's location based on your flight plan by the maps you have.

Depending on the winds, you sometimes had to go higher or lower, and you used to put out a call sign. When you got to a certain point, you gave your call sign out to tell other airplanes in the vicinity where you were because there were no traffic controllers. Some places may have had controllers, possibly just one, but most didn't. Back then, if you were going to fly over some African countries, many only had one radio, and it might not be working very well, so only the most basic information could be relayed.

The aircraft follows the flight plan from a fixed point to the following fixed point. The crew had to navigate themselves, talking back and forth with each other. They might say, "This is Fox Fox 544, just exiting a certain place at flight level 320, estimating, such and such at such and such." Everybody on that frequency could hear it, and quite often, someone would come back and say, "This is Air Afrique. We're at the same flight level. Would you like to go down or go up?"

They would respond, "Okay, we'll descend to 2000 feet below you so that you can see we're crossing paths." That was what you had to do. You had to act as your own air traffic controller.

You had to do it back then, and you still do it now in many places. When you get off the grid, it is a necessity. As you got into Africa, farther down near Nigeria, you used to often turn up at a major airport, call them, and have nobody pick up. Maybe, they were sleeping in the tower. Sometimes you had to circle for a while, waiting for someone to wake up and turn the landing lights on.

Then when you landed, so early in the morning, there was nobody there. You parked on the ramp around the corner and waited for your ground crew to turn up. Nobody was there and you would open up, and just listen to the jungle. You sat, and you sat. Everybody popped open a beer, and you sat there with your legs over the cargo door having a beer and waiting for workers to turn up. Eventually, workers would just come out from the bush and start unloading the airplane. Finally, a van with big orange lights used to take us out through the back road to the company house where we used to stay. Customs wasn't open that time of day.

The telex used to go out from London that, "Mr. Deakin is on board." Typically, the station manager would come out and meet me. Sometimes when I was down there, I would go through these small offices which contained nothing but a telex and a telephone.

It was the same in South America, but the temperature was the first thing you noticed in Africa when you got off an airplane — not a modern-day airplane.

The second thing was the smell. In Africa, Zambia comes to mind, the smell was very earthy, humid, tons of humidity. It was like opening an oven, and then somebody spraying you with a spray gun of water. And then all you heard in Africa was insects. Overwhelmingly noisy.

The experience was breathtaking.

For somebody who's never been before, it's not like going on vacation in the Caribbean or anything like that. It's entirely upside down.

And for a guy from Ramsgate going down into Africa for the first time, it was a complete sensory overload. My first time in Africa, I stayed at the IAS compound because I was meant to go back on another airplane, and there wasn't one going back. So, the station manager said, "Just crash with us tonight." I can still vividly remember driving down the street and seeing the reddish mud and people with huge loads balanced on their heads.

All the old buildings had these metal gratings around the wall to stop people from getting through into the building because that's Africa. They still have that now. It's just part of Africa. The railings were beautiful and ornate, but they could and did stop people from gaining access to the compound. They were clamped on the wall so people couldn't get in through windows.

This was in 1977, and I was nineteen years old.

All the airlines had their compounds in the same area. Air France and Air Afrique were next door. When you entered the compound, the first thing you noticed was a building with an eight-foot wall surrounding it and a security guard outside. Then the security guard would let you in and close the gate after you. Then, of course, they had a cook to do the meals for you, but there was a security guard inside, as well.

Then there was another metal gate between each bedroom.

Why?

Unfortunately, one day when another airline was out, some unsavory individuals came along with a truck, put a chain around the gate, and pulled the whole thing out of the wall. Then, they broke in and robbed the place.

On some occasions, if the electrical bill wasn't paid on time, the local electrical company would arrive, just take a pair of pliers and cut the wire.

The security guards weren't armed. They were just guards. But I must admit, the first time I saw the guards at the airport, standing by the airplane, I was quite shocked. Some were younger than me, fourteen or fifteen, dressed in Nigerian military uniform and carrying guns. That made me a bit nervous because I was thinking, "This guy's a kid. He's younger than me, and he's carrying a gun."

I had all kinds of experiences working with IAS Cargo.

One time, I nearly got arrested.

I went to see my parents and was sleeping because I had been working the night shift. Then, I got a call.

"Would you mind making the courier trip?"

I said, "Sure." Extra money, why not?

"Well, can you get up . . . we're going on our airplane tonight."

I drove back to Gatwick, got on the bus, and got on the airplane. And then when I arrived in Africa, I suddenly realized that my visa was invalid.

That wasn't a big problem. Not yet. So anyway, I completed that trip.

Two days later, I had another trip down there. This time, I flew down on a company airplane and was scheduled to return on the Caledonian. Unfortunately, I had forgotten that the visa on my passport wasn't up to date. So, as I was leaving Nigeria, I started to go through Immigration. The guy opened up my passport and said, "You don't have a valid visa."

I'm like, ". . . Yeah, I'm sorry. It ran out."

He replied, "No problem at all. Just get it next time around."

I went back to London, and then a week later, still without getting an updated visa, I went down on another flight. As I was going through Passport Control, with all these people crowded around, I saw this same guy. He looked at me and recognized me.

"Shit." It was the only thing I could think of at the time.

So, I went up to him, and they took me through customs. They wanted to lock me up in jail. I remember he said, "I told you not to come back here without it getting done."

I countered. "Can I call the station manager? We can get this handled."

We went down a labyrinth corridor of the brand-new airport they had just built, and I paid almost two hundred pounds buckshee money. I said, "Here, take this."

He said, "Right, no problem."

Three weeks later, still being the dumb shit that didn't get it done, I traveled on another airplane, one of our own down there. I came through the terminal to be cleared, and guess what? The same guy was on.

I went a whiter shade of pale and thought, "Oh my God. I got so busy with my life that I just didn't think about it."

That was when a Captain for an outbound Caledonian flight stepped in. He saw me with this guy, and he must have noticed the panic written all over my face.

He came over to me and said, "Hey, how are you?"

I replied, "Oh, great," as casually as possible.

Then he took me over to where his crew was gathered, and as we walked off, he started talking with me. As we rounded a corner, he immediately put one of the cabin attendant's jackets on me, took me to his Boeing 707 flight which I was scheduled to fly back to London on, and locked me in the cockpit of the airplane.

As I looked out from the cockpit, I saw the immigration officer and a guard with a gun. Both of them were looking for me. I flew straight back to Gatwick and got my passport taken care of. As soon as I hit the ground, I went to the authorities to get my passport updated. The passport was handed in to get a valid visa! If it hadn't been for that captain . . .

At IAS Cargo Airlines, I was one of two duty officers working my shifts. I wasn't allowed the scope and range that I enjoyed at Invicta International. I'd do everything I had to do, but nothing more. Invicta was more like being here in America where everything's possible, and you could make it happen. After working at IAS for a while, I began to feel that my wings were clipped.

I learned a lot, a hell of a lot at IAS . . . But I didn't feel like anyone was a team player. To me, the way IAS Cargo Airlines operated, even though it was so professional, something was missing, and I knew what it was. . .

Camaraderie.

IAS Cargo Airlines was my first worldwide airline. They were professional, a great airline, but too clinical.

I would often think of Hugh Kennard and all the people at Invicta. With Invicta International, I had a feeling of unity, excitement. It was more than an airline. It was a way of life. A privilege to work there. It was fun. Parts of IAS were great fun, but it was technical, not human.

Change isn't always personal, especially when it comes from an inside desire. Sometimes change is precipitated by outside pressures. A changing world. New economic considerations.

At the end of the 1970s, the world faced fuel embargos and the growing power of OPEC. 1979 was a horrendous time for any airline. Fuel prices escalated exponentially. In some cases, IAS cargo airlines could not get fuel and had to trade for fuel between various airlines.

On one occasion, we had an airplane returning from over Midway in the Pacific, and they didn't have any fuel. We couldn't find any fuel. We spoke to Pan Am, and whoever was coming that way, "Where do you need fuel? We'll trade." They would let us know where they needed fuel. Back then, you had a carna card used as a credit card, and if you did not have it, you were done. This was bread and butter. If your carna credit card got taken away due to non-payment, you were finished as an airline.

This fuel card was so valuable that it was kept locked in the cockpit. We continued to trade our fuel in other places. For example, another airline would say to us, "Okay. We need fuel at X location," which we might have. In exchange, they would allow us to use their fuel at the Y location. You knew which carriers were going through Midway, which carriers were going through different stations. So, you used to send them a Telex saying, "Hey, we've got an airplane going through there. We need this. Can we use this?" They would say, "Yes."

Then a second major paradigm shift occurred.

In 1979, the world's major airlines began to realize that instead of just putting baggage in the hold of their passenger plane, they could also carry mail and cargo. Airplanes going down to Africa, or wherever, started to make extra money by carrying freight.

This shift in thinking was a major blow to the strictly cargo airlines.

A two-pronged effect emerged.

The most significant aviation expenditures, crew, and fuel were rising and eroding at the possible profits. Then the wide-bodied planes started to come into service and load cargo as well as passengers. They completely blindsided the cargo airline business and collapsed the whole market.

The fuel embargo also put a lot of airlines out of business, including IAS. But by that time, I had already moved to my next adventure.

CHAPTER 4

Jersey Bound

"The desire to fly is an idea handed down to us by our ancestors who, in their grueling travels across trackless lands in prehistoric times, looked enviously on the birds soaring freely through space, at full speed, above all obstacles, on the infinite highway of the air." — Wilbur Wright

I WAS STILL WITH IAS cargo airlines when I learned of a position down at Intra Airways on the island of Jersey, where the Jersey cow comes from. It's a very quaint island, and they speak Jersey French, Patois French. Very quaint place. This was in 1979, and Intra was the main airline of Jersey.

I applied, and they invited me down for an interview. So, I drove to Bournemouth and got on this DC-3, the first time I had ever been in the DC-3. I was up in the cockpit with the crew, and I flew down to interview for the job. They used to fly cargo, produce, and everyday stuff, from England to Jersey, every night and every morning.

When I touched down, I had a feeling that the job might be a good fit. I remember going into Intra's office in Jersey and meeting this guy who was a policeman and a guard as well. He wore big thick glasses and was a very nice gentleman.

When I got there, he told me what the job was and what they did. He explained that although Intra flew cargo, it was primarily a passenger airline. I was intrigued because I'd never been involved with passengers before. Intra did a lot of passenger flights from all over Europe into Jersey. It was a big vacation point, bringing holiday makers in and out of Jersey and the Channel Islands.

I loved working at Intra Airways from the get-go. Intra combined the love of aviation that initially brought me to Invicta, with the professional efficiency of IAS Cargo, but on the passenger side. It was a good time. But then, I was back to doing everything again. I was back on course. I found my wings, and I was flying again.

On my first day on duty there, I wore my IAS Cargo Airline uniform because they didn't issue me a uniform, and I didn't have anything else. Everybody looked at me a little strange because they were dressed in civvies, not in uniforms.

The next day, one of the guys turned up with a uniform on just to take the piss out of me. But he ended up being quite okay.

The terminal was just across the road from the operations office. I would often go up in the tower, into the ATC control room, and watch the airplanes come in. We had Viscounts and DC-3s. Weekends were always the busiest because the flights brought people over or back for vacations.

On Friday nights, the fog would often roll in. I don't know why. Maybe because Friday was the busiest, most inconvenient time? Quite possibly.

The pilots were swashbuckling back then, which may be too strong a description, but probably because many of them had been fighter pilots. They were undoubtedly cavalier, for sure. But, nevertheless, when these pilots recognized a problem, they thought for themselves and came up with a solution.

The fog would stop traffic. Nobody could take off.

Did these pilots wait for the fog to lift?

No. With a fully loaded plane of passengers, they would taxi up and down the runway a couple of times with the engines going, in order to burn off the fog and allow for maximum clearance visibility to take off.

Who'd think about doing that now?

Now, everyone would just sit and wait for the fog to clear. Right? Can you imagine any captain saying, "Ladies and gentlemen, we're just going to run up and down the runway to clear the fog." But, of course, no one would consider doing anything like that. They would just sit at the gate and let everybody wait.

But that was what these pilots were like. Everybody had a great time because they wanted to make things happen.

I finished training for my pilot's license there at the Jersey Flying Club. My flying instructor was an amazing fellow, who used to call me "Mrs. Deakin's little boy."

When I got things wrong — and when you are training as a pilot in the airplane, you almost always get a few things wrong — he had very pointed ways of making me remember what I should be doing. If I didn't keep my hand on the throttle, he would take the handheld microphone and whack me with the thing.

"Now, that hurt, didn't it?" he would admonish.

I replied, "Yes."

"Now you're not going to forget not to put your hand on there again. Are you?"

Being the quick study that I am, I shook my head, "No, I'm not going to do that again. Sir."

The man was an absolute terror, but he did build that muscle memory in the brain. I never forgot it. My hand stays on the throttle with a clear memory of how much being hit on the hand hurt.

The Jersey Flying Club was also a focal local meeting place. Everybody used to go down to the club after work every night. Flight crews, cabin crews, everybody from all the airlines were down there. This place, jam-packed with assortments of alcoholic beverages flowing, the establishment used to be known as forward ops. If the control tower wanted us, they would always be sure to find us if they called by phone.

Across the road was a company house where they used to board crews and personnel. When I first lived there, working on Sundays was difficult for me, to be quite honest, because I would sometimes have a bit too much on Saturday nights at the Flying Club.

But I was the one who started up the whole airline in the morning, and I was supposed to arrive at 5:30 a.m.

I did set my alarm. However, by 5:00 a.m., or maybe 4:45 a.m., the alarm went off for about the fifth time. My eyes would open up, with circles underneath, looking like they'd just seen Mars five times. "Christ. I've got to be there!"

I would leap up, get in the car, drive like a bat out of hell around the corner. All the flight crews would be outside, waiting. They'd tap their feet or their watches and say, "Little boy having too much fun last night, were we?"

"No, sir." I replied although I was unconvincing. What would you do?

"Well, guess what, young man? You're buying the beer tonight."

I met many lifelong friends there, and the experience contributed to my aviation education. Many of the people I worked with went global from Jersey. They're all over the world now.

That was where I met Joe Rediger. Joe probably was about five foot, two inches, in a dark blue uniform, Captain stripes, and a smart Intra Jersey cap. Joe was nearly up for retirement, so I think he was in his early fifties when I first met him. He had a crinkly face, crafty smile, an elegant twinkle in his eyes, and history. When you looked at him, you could see the history.

Joe worked for Intra Airways when I was in Jersey. He flew the DC-3s and lived in Jersey. He was a fighter pilot during World War II, and I mean, he could tell a story. One story he told was about when they were flight training.

"In those days," he said, "when you were flight training, you just followed the leader."

On one particular day, when they were following the leader, that rule was taken to the extreme. A couple of airplanes in front of him just plowed into the ground because the lead aircraft was too low, and they were just "following the leader."

Joe was there at the root of aviation. He was an art form in aviation, very much part of the beginning, of how things were done. He was good at what he did because aviation was ingrained in him.

One morning as we walked to the awaiting DC-3, he walked up to the aircraft, looked at it, and said, "That's overweight."

"How can you say that?" I would ask.

He could tell just by looking at the tires and the pressure on the tires. He would know how much cargo was on the plane, and he could tell if it was overweight. He could just look at it and tell by the way the airplane sat if the cargo was in the nose or too much in the back. His experience had evolved to the point where he knew just by looking at the airplane.

I flew with Joe any chance I could get, and he was highly professional but extremely fun. I can remember one occasion where we were taxiing out from Jersey, and all these aircraft were taxiing out to go to the runway too. One plane came around the corner from the first ramp, and another plane was going around the corner from a second ramp. The controller was stuck and didn't know what to do. It was not the controller's fault, or anybody's fault, that these airplanes were now facing each other and would have to wait for tugs to come out. Joe was so professional and said, "No problem."

Dear old Joe, he just pulled up the throttle and taxied across the grass because you can do that in a DC-3. He taxied across the grass, off to the runway he went. There was a big chuckle all around among everybody else. He said, "Well, there you go."

That was the type of character he was: a scholar, a gentleman, and a master of his art.

Intra's fleet consisted of smaller airplanes transporting holidaymakers, and some things were quite different than IAS Cargo. Other missions, different times. This experience was all about the passengers. We had check-in desks, the whole lot. It was my first indoctrination into a passenger airline. But the one thing that I couldn't fathom was the different method for scheduling the crews.

At IAS, they had a crew plot, a big board on the wall going all the way out months ahead with the same flight numbers used to assign the crew, Captain Johnson, Captain whatever. From that, the crewing person at IAS would then say, okay, we need these people here for the crew. How do we get them out? Well, put them on Lufthansa. Put them on Air France. We're putting them on Air Afrique.

But at Intra, it was nothing like that.

Each day we had to plot fresh crew assignments. And so, we would manually call all the crew members between 5:00 and 6:00 p.m. every night and give them their flight schedule, what they were doing the next days. They had to wait or have a trusted someone wait for the call, but somebody had to be by the phone to pick it up. So, the crews never knew their schedule until 5:00 or 6:00 the night before. They didn't even know if they were off.

Weird, right? This was running in a regular airline.

At night, Intra operated the paper runs. The plane's interior was taken out to make room for the newspaper run to the islands for the next day. We would bring in *The Telegraph, The Times*, whatever.

I stumbled into my first-ever charter experience while I was at Intra Airways. It was completely by accident, without permission, and I had no idea I was even doing it at the time. I was working in operations about 8:00 p.m., and a British Caledonian BAC-1-11 was taxiing out, all ready to go — their last scheduled flight of the day to London.

I could see the runway from our office, hear the plane quite clearly, and as the plane got to the end of the runway and started an engine run up for liftoff, there was a huge bang.

I thought, "Oh, shit. They've lost an engine."

Sure enough, this plane came back on the ramp.

My mind was racing, and I thought, "Huh. We have a Viscount outside. We could use that plane and help them out."

So, I called British Caledonian and said, "Hey, your schedule Jersey — London flight just lost an engine on takeoff. Can we help you fly these passengers up?"

They came back right away and said, "Sure. What have you got?" I said, "We've got a Viscount available. We'll just put your passengers on there and fly them to their destination."

Now, airlines cancel flights left, right, and center, but not then. We generally had crews on standby. I called our standby and asked, "Hey, do you want to do a quick fly-up to London?"

The response was enthusiastic and immediate. The entire crew made it to the airport in about thirty minutes. We had the airplane rounded up, passengers on board, got the engineers going, and it was gone.

That was my first-ever charter flight.

I remember coming into the office the next day, and the commercial manager came up to me and said, "Crickey, Tracey, good job." I didn't realize what I had done. I honestly didn't.

I mean, it was crazy. We didn't talk money. There was no money exchanged. We didn't talk about anything. We just launched the airplane and left it to commercial to sort out the details the next day.

At the end of '79, Jersey European purchased Intra, and the airline pretty much folded or was turned over. Everybody who was part of Intra was let go. Intra as we knew it just completely stopped. The new company renamed the airline Jersey European.

I don't know why I didn't reapply to Jersey European, but I didn't.

So, I was out of work during a difficult time. The aviation world was upside down with increased fuel prices and embargos. World economies were grappling with recession. We were tied to foreign gas, and airlines were going bust all over the place.

I wrote letters, left, right and center. I didn't know what exactly I was going to do. Trying to get a position in aviation, even with my experience, was extremely difficult.

Many things were changing. As I mentioned, all the airline companies that used to put cargo upstairs were now starting to put cargo in the hold down underneath the plane. Usually, those holds were empty, so this was an earth-shattering change — a completely new way of doing things.

I knew I wanted to stay in aviation, and I was always looking for another challenge. When I reflect on this time in my life, I view everything I did before the establishment of Le Bas International as building blocks, one stepping stone leading to another stepping stone.

Then, a company called Fairflight showed some interest in me out of the blue and invited me out for an interview. They were based at Biggin Hill, and I remember meeting them at an office in a hangar. They told me about a new company that they wanted to get going.

CHAPTER 5

Air Mail

"Let's get one thing straight. There's a big difference between a pilot and an aviator. One is a technician; the other is an artist in love with flight." — Elrey Borge Jeppesen

F AIRFLIGHT HAD A RELATIONSHIP with Air Ecosse, a Scottish commuter airline based in Aberdeen. Air Ecosse also carried out mail flights for the Royal Mail, the European equivalent of Datapost.

I knew about mail and cargo airlines, small executive airplanes, passenger airlines, and acting as a courier. I was hired to put the dots together to start Fairflight/Air Ecosse's London-base on behalf of Datapost.

At the time, I didn't realize that Datapost would develop into what is now known as Parcelforce, which is a vast organization responsible for mail in the United Kingdom. Sometimes you don't realize how your work will evolve. You don't see how far-reaching it can become.

When I first started with Fairflight/Air Ecosse, we had one Embraer aircraft. Within the space of three months, we were up to fourteen aircraft. For the first time, the British public could write a letter in the morning, and it would be delivered the next day. Since Air Ecosse was contracted to fly Datapost, some of the airplanes were literally painted red to look like the mail truck with Dataposts on the side for decoration.

During the day, the airline flew passengers around on scheduled service. We would use a great, big freight door to remove the plane's interior to ship high-priority mail at night.

Yes, I set up that operation. We were based in the old Court Line building in Luton Airport, London in Bedfordshire. Court Line was a 20th-century British shipping company that was founded in 1905. In the 1960s, it diversified into shipbuilding, charter aviation, and was the very first airline to operate the Tri-Star. In addition, the building housed a wind tunnel that they used as a base to test jet engines in the early 1970s.

There was a huge parking ramp outside where we used to park all the airplanes, all fourteen of them eventually.

We were in their main building. Mail trucks from all over London used to hand the mail off to the duty person for the post office who would then use the old Court Line building as a sorting station. Then the mail would go to airplanes bound for Birmingham, Manchester, Aberdeen, Glasgow, Edinburgh, East, Midlands, Northern Ireland, etc.

I was opening doors and throwing mail into the airplanes. Well, maybe not throwing mail into the aircraft. "Placing mail" would be the right way to say it. I placed mail into the airplanes and sent them off with a turnaround of thirty-five minutes or less.

In, out, and gone.

The postmaster general and his teams used to arrive and help off-load and load the mail onto the planes themselves. Boom — door open, close in, out, gone.

Why the quick turnaround?

Because these same airplanes had to be back the following day, on time and ready for their scheduled 7:00 am passenger flight.

I kept a strict timetable. Those airplanes didn't just depart. They departed on time. "The door is closing. We've got to go." I may have sounded a bit harsh, but this was an era of "Pull your socks up, young man." Stiff upper lip and get on with it.

The planes would arrive about 7:00 in the evening, with the last one coming in at 11:00 p.m., possibly a bit later than that. Then we had to clean up and go home. So, I used to finish roughly about two to three o'clock in the morning.

At the same time, I was also still flying for Volkswagen. Ted Cooper, VW Chief Pilot for the UK, used to fly out of Cranfield because the airplane had been moved there. When I finished at Datapost in the wee hours, I would drive thirty minutes from Luton to Cranfield airport and fly with Ted to Germany and back. I grabbed about two hours of sleep each way, then returned the next morning and repeated the process all over again.

I was a dedicated idiot sleeping in two separate two-hour shifts each night for pittance pay.

But that's where sheepdogging comes in! Sheepdogging is my management style, and it was starting to develop during this time of intense work and experience.

What is sheepdogging?

Try to imagine what a sheepdog does. The dog is out in the field or prairie, and the shepherd has a whistle to maneuver the sheepdog around the sheep as he puts them into a pen. Now, if it weren't for the sheepdog continuously homing in on the sheep, not letting them go, pushing them in the right direction, guiding them this way and that, encouraging them into the pen where they will be taken care of, then the sheep would escape. They would run away, and just go wherever.

That same principle goes for clients.

If you want to keep your clients, sheepdog them because if you let the operation run on automatic, where will the sheep go?

In aviation, if you're not on time, you're not going to get customers. And if you don't offer good service, you're not giving value for return. That ties into sheepdogging.

When you speak with a client who needs a problem to be solved, you have to perform. If somebody wants something by a specific time, you give it to them by a particular time. In fact, you do even better than that. You give it to them early. If I promise something by a certain time, then I'll give it to you earlier.

That's why I call my management style sheepdogging.

Because you have to sheepdog every single client, and that's not a bad thing. You can turn that into something positive. If you're not answering those persistent, picky questions, then the client may be thinking, "I don't really want to do that. Or even work with these people."

If you don't constantly look after your clients, especially when you don't know them, then you must make a conscious effort to keep in contact with them. You need to keep availing yourself to them. If they have other questions, then make sure that the questions are answered. It helps, I say, to put their concerns back in the pen. Do you see the approach?

That's the whole philosophy if you want it in a nutshell. It's my total philosophy of customer care and customer service. Period. This is it. It doesn't matter what else you do.

If you don't keep a close eye on and close contact with the client, they will roam. If you look at a piece that's straying away, even on a website or a blog or whatever, if you look at that, and you say, "Does that really hit the key, does it really get it?" And if you can't answer straight away, then you're not delivering your mission to the client. You're not saying to the client, "Hey, this is an offer I have for you that might be of interest." You're allowing the client, inviting the client, even giving the client permission to look elsewhere. In everything you do, you have to look at your actions in the same respect.

Managing employees is part of sheepdogging too. Over the years, we've had many people join the company, and every single one of them has been taught the sheepdogging skill. Even our president, Donough Hughes, learned that.

sheepdogging is like a toolbox. So please bring it to everybody you know. That's what I've tended to do over my life.

When I was younger, I used to hold onto the information in the following manner - I have something valuable and you don't.

But that's wrong.

You learn over time that the information you have grows outwards.

That it's kind of like a plant with seeds. If a plant can't let go of its seeds and put them elsewhere, it's not going to grow and have other plants. That's the same with information. If you don't share information and use it, the information held is a waste of time. Information shared is powerful.

Recognize who the client is and what their needs are. But, again, with the Internet and every other type of electronic communication and technique, you've got to remember that you have a human being behind it.

All this boils down to the principles of making sure that it's right, making sure it's on time, and ensuring the service is given professionally. So, my advice to anybody is: Be polite, be professional, and be timely. That's it.

Serendipity is often the ultimate irony. If I had not been working that round the clock schedule at Datapost, I would not have connected with Gerry Bron and his company, Executive Express.

Of course, at the time, I didn't know anything about them. I was simply working the airplanes in the Court Line building, which was right next to the Executive Express hangar.

The Executive Express office personnel used to come up and see me when they were finishing their workday. Everyone there was headed home, but our ramp at night was bustling with activity and packed with mail trucks. They couldn't believe the number of airplanes congregated there.

The Executive Express commercial guy saw our aircraft coming in and out, and I noticed their fleet of 421 Golden Eagles and Cessna 404 Titans. He came up one day and started chatting with me.

He asked, "Why don't you come over tomorrow to our building, just when you can, and I'll introduce you to everybody." I didn't even recognize this as an interview.

The following morning, after my flights to Germany and the drive back from Cranfield, I went over to the Executive Express office. As I walked into the building, the interior made an immediate impression on me. Everything was so lovely, very James Bond-ish. To the left of the entrance was the VIP lounge, all plush, with excellent lighting, plants, and art on the walls. Executive Express attendants, all nicely dressed, served elegant clients their morning coffee and little bakery items.

I thought I had walked into the wrong place.

I asked for the guy I spoke with the day before and was shown upstairs to his office. And he started talking about how my experience was such a good fit because they were flying Cessna 404 Titans, precisely the same airplane that I was flying for Volkswagen.

And so, he asked me to speak to the main post office person about applying to get two runs from Datapost. I introduced them, and eventually, Executive Express got the Bristol and Dublin runs. Yeah. Bristol and Dublin. The Dublin route was the first outside of the United Kingdom.

A couple of weeks later, I was offered a job with Executive Express. I was initially reluctant because I had just set up Datapost and had been with them only about five months. But he persisted. He wanted me to load up their airplanes for the Datapost run each night, which would be two planes compared to fourteen. Not only that, but the manager wanted me to continue to fly with Executive Express as a safety pilot and work in ops as well. Oh, and they were going to pay me more money.

Okay, so what's wrong with that picture?

I found my Datapost replacement and started meeting lots of new people and executives that I would associate with later in my career. Executive Express was a fixed base operations (FBO) airport business that handled private aviation, aircraft passengers, and other services such as fueling, hangaring, tie-down and parking, aircraft rental, maintenance, and flight instruction. We call them handling agents in Europe, and they're called FBOs over here in the US.

Executive Express had an impressive corporate fleet at the time: Beechcraft King Airs, Cessna Citations, 404 Titans and Golden Eagle 421s. They were among the first to have lounge areas specifically designed for the customer's comfort. These weren't just a simple coffee area, but very plush and cutting edge.

For me, this was a step into a different world.

Executive Express was my introduction to Gerry Bron. Gerry was a leader in the rock and roll music industry in the United Kingdom. He was the sharp end of it, a record producer and band manager of some of the most popular bands of the time: Uriah Heep, Manfred Mann, Motorhead, The Alan Parsons Project, and many others. In addition, Alan Parson did a lot of work with Pink Floyd on their Dark Side of the Moon album.

Gerry started buying planes out of pure necessity. He was managing so many different bands and moving them around so much that he thought he might as well get his own airplanes. Then to keep the planes and the pilots busy with full-time work, Gerry started the Executive charter business. He continued to handle the music side of the company, and Executive Express took care of the charter business, moving the bands and other celebrities and executives.

The first time I met Gerry, I was asked to deliver a package to the main office in Bron Records' roundhouse. I said, "Sure." I didn't realize that Gerry was in the music industry. So, I got talking away with him, and he showed me around the music studio. I had never seen a music studio before. He showed me how they could change the drum beat just by using the dials on the soundboard. I was like, "Holy crap. That's how it's done?" I thought it was amazing. It looked like the cockpit of an airplane, but for a music person.

If I hadn't met Gerry Bron, I wouldn't have met anyone in the music industry. If I hadn't met music people, we wouldn't have learned how to move artists and their tours around, or the correct way to load the band staff in the front and the band equipment in the back of the plane.

We wouldn't be doing business for many of the music celebrities that we work with today.

I went to work for Executive Express to gain experience working with luxury passenger charters, and that led me to music people, and eventually down the trail to our business relationship with Live Nation. A long and winding road. There's a thread through it all.

I remember flying out very late this one night on our way to Brussels. We were going to pick up the master tapes from one of the executives from Gerry's record label, Bronze Records, and bring them back to London. I was pretty overwhelmed that we were going to get those tapes. The masters were the tapes that they used to make the records. So, to me, it was like, "Whoa!" He opened my eyes up to possibilities in the music industry.

If it hadn't been for Gerry, I wouldn't have been introduced to the music world and the world of celebrity.

Through Executive Express, I got to meet music people, race car drivers, professional people. I connected with record producers, tour managers, and artists.

I used to sit there in the lounge and have coffee with these people in these little coffee cups. Of course, I had to pinch myself sometimes, but I became comfortable with it. No problem at all. It didn't matter who they were. They were just people.

So many beautiful people came through the Executive Express because it was a class act in Luton. I met one race car driver who turned up with his Learjet one day. He was a nice guy, but he had been badly burned in a racing accident.

Niki Lauda loved flying. I remember him coming through Luton, and he was a pleasure. He would shake your hand. He was polite, just an honorable fellow. I met quite a few Formula One racing drivers over the years, but he was exceptional, very technical, and precise when you spoke to him. He knew exactly what he wanted, but he was private and intelligent. His mind was very mechanical.

That experience helped me move into the executive realm, understand what executives expect, what entertainers need, what professionals require. I mean, the world is more demanding of them now. The money is so significant when entertainers go on tour today. They've got to be ready, prepared. Everything has got to be really tight.

Otherwise, everything gets completely messed up. The tour business was slightly more lackadaisical in those days.

Pink Floyd was our first-ever band booking here in the United States with Le Bas International. That was our first extensive world tour. The booking came about via a gentleman whose partner left to start his own company. We were doing other business with this gentleman when he said, "I've got this tour coming up for Pink Floyd over in the States. Can you help out?"

Le Bas International sourced the airplane for the band, the singers, the technicians, the setup team, everybody. About 123 people, or thereabouts.

CHAPTER 6

Not a Good Fit

"Learn from the mistakes of others. You won't live long enough to make all of them yourself." — Eleanor Roosevelt

A FTER WORKING WITH EXECUTIVE Express, I spent a short time with a company called Redcoat Air Cargo. I heard somebody say the company was looking for somebody in their operations department, and I thought, "Why not?"

Redcoat was quite well known because their airplane was used in Buccaneer, a TV series in the UK and the fictional airline was known as Redair. The plot centered around swashbuckling people who were living from paycheck to paycheck. The hero in the show mortgaged his house to get his airline going, and the weekly episodes revolved around the adventures of the airplane crew as they traveled to and from Africa.

What I figured out pretty soon after I began there was that Redcoat Air Cargo was being run like the television show.

Of course, I didn't know this at first. The airline flew the Bristol Britannia, and I loved the airplane. I was very familiar with how it operated. I already knew about overflights, traffic landing rights, getting permits, and all that stuff.

The person who interviewed me was familiar with my background with the airplane and already understood that I had a lot of experience with freight cargo. I had worked for one of the biggest cargo companies in the United Kingdom.

But it wasn't a good fit. I was uncomfortable there from day one. You know, it's like when you walk into something, and you've accepted a position, and the first thing you say to yourself is, "Why did I do this?"

I oversaw the operation when I was on duty, but the company was being run on a shoestring. The money that they made from each charter was paying for everything else. There was no buffer behind it. I mean, they were surviving from paycheck to paycheck, and they were barely making it. I could see that they were a company that was destined to go out of business.

Later, when I was with Zambia Airways and getting my feet wet in the charter business with my first company, Transcontinental Systems, I ran into the chairman of Redcoat again. The company had folded, and he was trying to start a charter service. The only difference was I was barely twenty, and he was well over that.

With Redcoat, I think I was caught by a certain feeling of longing to return to my early days when I was at Invicta. Perhaps that influenced my decision to work there, but in the end, it just didn't feel right, and I acknowledged that. Redcoat was a disaster waiting to happen.

I checked with Flight International, a magazine that lists pretty much all available openings in aviation. From an operations manager friend who worked at Alidair, I got a job with them up in East Midlands. The mood was completely different, much more enjoyable, and fun. They had a sales department, and they did quite a lot of music engagements.

Alidair was owned by a packaging company in the United Kingdom, and that was where they got their operating money. They had their main base down in East Midlands and others in Aberdeen and Guernsey. So Alidair, Guernsey Airlines, and its business link with British Midland were all different parts of a one-in-the-same-company.

At the time, the discovery of oil in the North Sea was emerging as a gamechanger. Helicopters would take personnel out to the oil rigs, but they only had enough fuel to go so far. So, they built a substantial airport in the Shetlands, up north of Scotland. Three or four times a day, Alidair used to fly from Aberdeen up to the Shetlands with oil people. From there, the helicopters were used to ferry personnel out to the oil rigs in the North Sea.

The crews used to go out to the rigs for a month, come back, and go out a month again. We positioned people and had a contract with Conoco, one of the more prominent fuel companies, to take people out there.

We did it all.

We moved ships and crews around, as well as conducted scheduled service for British Midland Airlines. The company had ties back to Invicta because Hugh Kennard started British Midland and was an active partner. So here was the theme once again, aviation as a small circle in a big world.

Alidair had the contract. When the Short 330 aircraft, a small turboprop that would seat up to thirty passengers, was introduced, we would use it to fly in between East Midlands and London Heathrow. We also did a scheduled Edinburgh service and an Aberdeen service.

Because these oil folks needed frequent transit back and forth to London Heathrow, our service became the first real air connection between the Midlands and the rest of the United Kingdom.

In addition to the scheduled service, we also ran charters. I traveled all over Europe on those charter flights. I especially enjoyed the music charters, like Kid Creole and the Coconuts. At that time, I was also doing safety pilot flying for BAC Leasing, an aircraft charter company, on their Embraer EMB 110 Bandeirante airplane.

I was privileged to meet some interesting people, like the family founders of Scholl Shoes. I was also able to land at these airports out in the Shetland Islands.

That was the first time I bumped into Barry Manilow. I can remember picking him up in East Midlands one snowy day. I saw this guy coming around the corner, walking towards us. He had an oversized fur coat on and a kind of a beaky nose. I thought, "What's that coming towards us?" I didn't know who Barry Manilow was; I had no idea. I didn't know who a lot of these people were. My brain was gobbling up all the experiences, all these people, so many stories.

In England, as in America, the time zones change every year, and our crews would never get there at the right time in the morning. So, you would be sitting there with the passengers and the lights going on saying, "Where's the first officer?"

"I can't find him."

"What?"

He was in a different time zone.

So, I had to drive across fields in a Land Rover to get the guy out of bed, pick him up, and get him into the airplane. Crazy stuff!

Then Alidair's commercial director left, and the company's commercial work began to fade. Another employee took over the position, but he wasn't bringing as much commercial work as needed, so the company suffered. The main thing that kept the company going was the oil business.

I remember that everyone was on tenterhooks wondering if Alidair would get another extension of the oil contract. It did. But the company was so worried that it might not, they began to move personnel around, and their actions accelerated a growing perception that the company was going backwards, not forwards.

I was always thinking about the big question: "Is this company going to be here?" And with the rumor mill of suspicion circulating, I was determined not to get caught on the outs again, as I had before. My goal was a job in aviation, and at the time, I was being pulled from all different angles.

I started writing inquiry letters to various airlines. And by then, I knew that I wanted to go back to the central hub, the airports in London. I applied to every London contact I could think of, every company based at a London airport: Air India, Singapore Airlines, Qantas, Swiss Air, Scandinavian Airlines, Iberia, Air France, Pan-American, etc. Unfortunately, all of those jobs were highly sought-after jobs.

During the time Alidair was downsizing, I was moved to Aberdeen to take care of the oil flights. But as soon as I got there, the job reminded me of what I used to do with Fairflight and Air Ecosse. The similarities were all too clear and I was not happy with it. I was bored doing flights, and I felt transported back to the bench under the tree at boarding school. I would see our Alidair flights going to London or East Midland, and all I could think of was, "I want to get on that airplane and go." I felt as if I was moving in reverse.

I attended briefings from postal chief personnel when I worked for Air Ecosse. After the session, I'd usually finish a night shift and then take the very last airplane back to the head office in Aberdeen. So, I used to get on the aircraft and fly with Bandeirante as a safety pilot. That's where I first got to know the Bandeirante, sitting in the copilot seat and flying with them to Aberdeen.

There was a bed-and-breakfast place there where we stayed. We would get there at about five-thirty in the morning, sleep till ten o'clock, and then go to the meeting in the office in Aberdeen. Afterward, I would get back on the same airplane and fly to Luton to start the whole thing over again.

I was not conflicted about staying in Aberdeen. I wanted out, but in hindsight, this was exactly where I needed to be at this point in time. If it hadn't been for this experience, I would not be where I am now. My future would have been completely different. Massively changed. Yet, I found the experience incredibly depressing. Yes, there it is . . . bottomless depressing. This was the same down feeling I had when I left Datapost and went to Executive Express.

After Alidair, a couple of airlines asked me for interviews. I would hop a flight on my days off and go down to interview, then come back the next night and return to work. Of all the interviews, El Al Israeli Airlines at London Heathrow came through and offered me the job. I went to work for them in their customer service department, handling customers at the check-in and transit desks.

What I learned from El Al Israeli Airlines was security.

Security is paramount with them. Persecution, past and present, made the airline cognizant that protecting their passengers had to be a priority if they wanted to stay in business. Perhaps "protect "is not the right word. Maybe "vigilant" is the word I should use.

They must be vigilant at all times, so I learned their systems and how their security systems work. A security officer does not let that aircraft out of their sight until the plane takes off again. Every single moment, every step of the way, there was not a person or a piece of baggage on an airplane that was not monitored. They were very efficient, and I assure you, it was like herding a bunch of cats into a box. I was amazed, and I still am amazed to this very day, at how the process was thoroughly thought out, every step of the way, all the way through.

El Al said that if you don't mention security, you don't have a security problem; and as soon as you say security, you've got a security problem, so don't mention it. We use the same approach to channel some of our guests, especially those in the public domain, heads of state, diplomats, celebrities. You can move well-known personalities around airports, and the general populace just won't know who they are. We've learned to adapt the procedures because of that one fact, which came from my experience with El Al Israeli Airlines.

I'd never been through any experience as singular as helping Israeli passengers. They are the most high-energy, fervent, and sometimes argumentative people on the planet. Before they even approached the desk, they would have to go through security. Security was part of the embassy, and so, they were asked some questions. I mean, really tight stuff before they came to the check-in desk.

If they hadn't been checked in right, you had to send them back. But many of them used to turn up with a busload of baggage and then tried to tell me that they only had one piece of carry-on luggage! They used to be passionate, and challenging. So, I would have to lay down the law and say, "Sir, you either have to check it, or you're not going. What do you want to do? Security, can you get the next person?"

That usually brought them around. "No, no, no, no. It's okay. We'll do it."

That took care of security, but I had customers who did that every day. I worked for El Al Israeli Airlines for two years.

If someone were to ask my opinion, "Would you like to have flown Pan American going to Israel? Or would you like to have gone on El Al Israeli Airlines?" I would say that on Pan American, you would have had excellent service. On El Al, they weren't known for their service. It wasn't bad, but when you got on El Al, you knew the plane was safe. No question. Safe and secure.

There are so many checks. When an El Al airplane lands anywhere in the world, it is one hundred percent safe. Wherever it lands, a security officer does not leave visual, does not leave that airplane until it takes off again.

Because I was not an Israeli citizen, my contract with the airline could only last for ten months. Then I had to take two months off because I was a UK citizen. That was how the airline was able to employ people like me seasonally as a part-time employee.

When I knew that the ten-month deadline was coming up, I was again asking, "What am I going to do for two months before I can come back?" And sometimes, you didn't know if you were going to get a contract back. You were not promised that, although it was likely that you would be re-employed. However, there was always that slim possibility you wouldn't get rehired.

During that time, I heard through Flight International about BAC Leasing. They were looking for a person to help them out in operations and also to fly as a safety pilot. And guess what they were doing at night?

The mail run out of London Gatwick.

When I interviewed with them, I was in the office for fifteen minutes when the guy said, "Hey, you want to start tonight?"

I answered, "Sure, I'll start tonight, no problem." Boom.

During this uncertain, exasperating time, I often asked myself why I stuck with it?

But I always knew the answer as I asked the question. The most important ingredient in my life at that time, and all the way up to the present, was my passion for aviation and aerospace. The passion is the heat. The passion is the sword, the hot rod, the rocket, the explosion—all of that. The passion and the desire create the way forward. There you go. Said it. It's been the nucleus of everything I've done.

As human beings, our frustration creates change. Therefore, discover what you don't like. It will enable you to move forward and find your true path. My philosophy is if you have the same ice cream every day, and you don't taste another ice cream, how do you know what the other ice creams taste like?

What does it take to make the decision to stay in your chosen field no matter what?

If I think about aviation, I see it as a passion that evolves like a flower. And the reason why I'm good at it is because I like it, and I keep doing it.

I work at it because I know it. It's not because I've been forced to do any of this. It's because I do it every day and I don't look at this as a business. I look at aviation and aerospace as fun.

East Midlands Airport (EMA). G-ANCF Bristol Britannia was one of two aircraft Invicta International owned: G-ANCF and G-AOVF, 1979. (*Photo courtesy Dick Gilbert*)

Tracey Deakin in the pilot seat of Invicta International's Bristol Britannia—as per historical sales literature at the time fondly referred to as The Whispering Giant 321 G-ANCF— at Manston Airport, (MSE) Kent, UK.

G-VWGB. Cessna 404 Titan. Glasgow International Airport (GLA). At the time, speciality registrations were unknown. European air traffic controllers always commented, inquiring "if the aircraft was related to Volkswagen." (*Photo Courtesy Paul Thallon*)

IAS Cargo Airlines, callsign FF. Seen here: McDonnell Douglas DC-8-54F G-BSKY. London Stansted (STN) IAS Cargo Airlines merged with TMAC on 15 August 1979 to create British Cargo Airlines, which began trading under its new name five days later. The merged entity's fleet comprised 15 aircraft, including eight DC-8 jet freighters, six CL-44-D, and one CL-44-0 turboprop freighter. (*Photo Courtesy Simon Barker*)

Intra Airways McDonnell Douglas DC-3. "DC" stands for Douglas Commercial. The DC-3 had many exceptional qualities compared to previous aircraft. It was fast, had a good range, was more reliable, and carried passengers in greater comfort. Lovable registered G-AMPY Staverton Airport (GLO). (*Photo Courtesy Simon Barker*)

Air Ecosse (parent company Fairflight Charters) was a Scottish commuter airline based in Aberdeen (ABZ) that operated Embraer Bandeirante EMB110. The company established the Royal Mail's Datapost air network, London Luton (LTN), as the primary hub. G-DATA outside Executive Express hangar (LTN). In the background is the tail of G-BRIT, Cessna 421 Golden Eagle, owned by Britannia Airways and managed by Executive Express (LTN) to ferry flight crews. (*Photo Courtesy Fergal Goodman*)

Tracey Deakin in one of BAC Leasing's London Gatwick (LGW) Embraer EMB110 – Safety Pilot.

Euroair Embraer EMB110 (G-MOBL). Late-night passenger safety pilot duty. Amsterdam, Schiphol (AMS), parked next to KLM Fokker 27 CityHopper.

Zambia Airways McDonnell Douglas DC-10-30 N3016Z (YUM) maiden and delivery flight to Zambia. (*Photo Courtesy McDonnell Douglas/Zambia Airways*)

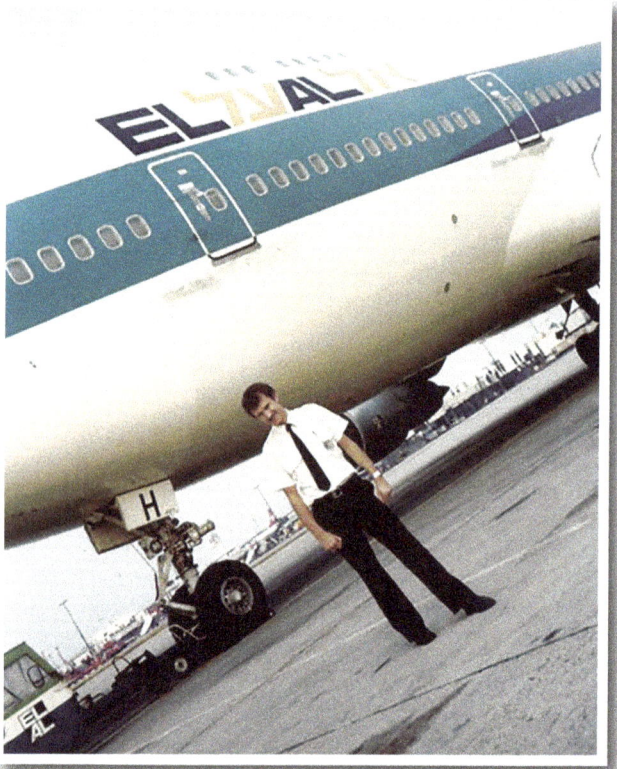

Tracey and an EL AL Israel Airlines Boeing, 747-200 (4X-AXH). London, Heathrow (LHR), UK.

CHAPTER 7

Return to Africa

"Within all of us is a varying amount of space lint and stardust,
the residue from our creation. Most are too busy to notice it, and
it is stronger in some than others. It is strongest in those of us who
fly and is responsible for an unconscious, subtle desire to slip into
some wings and try for the elusive boundaries of our origin."

— K.O. Eckland

W HEN ZAMBIA AIRWAYS ADVERTISED for an operations specialist with aviation experience, I applied for the position. At the time, I was on hiatus from El Al Israeli Airlines and flying for BAC, and I remember seeing the listing in the back of Flight International and deciding, "Okay, I'll apply for that." The position with Zambia Airways sounded interesting, and it would be an opportunity to return to Africa.

I was invited down to their main offices in Piccadilly for the interview.

As they started talking with me, I remember thinking that the vibe was easy and relaxed. I didn't realize the job was a slam-dunk because I had experience with Africa and aviation.

Before I even left the office, they offered me the position. But as I walked out, I asked, "How many people applied?" They replied, "About four hundred fifty."

"Wow." I was a little floored.

At London Heathrow Airport, Zambia Airways had an area

manager, a station manager, and a district manager. We took care of the whole operations and got on very well. The other managers and I set up all the necessary stations, such as checking in passengers, baggage, anything to do with arrivals and departures, the whole lot. We did everything, from loading passengers to load control to get-the-cargo-on-the-airplanes. Throughout the stations, I was doing everything, so I learned everything.

But the most exciting aspect of the job was that I would be asked to work stints down into Africa and given assignments to outstations. For example, if we were opening service to a place where there was no outlet for Zambia Airways, we used to go ahead to the site to set everything up.

Kenneth Kaunda was the president of the country of Zambia at the time. He used to have this white handkerchief that he would take out of his pocket and wave at everybody. That was his signature.

We also used to go ahead and set up head-of-state and presidential visits as well. The planning involved a lot of different details that combined other areas of my aviation experience, including handling freight, passengers, first-class expectations, checking, and ticketing into one unified package.

These were regular scheduled services. The network started on Monday night when Zambia's flagship, the McDonnell Douglas DC-10 would travel from London to Lusaka. Tuesday, the aircraft would fly from Lusaka to Larnaca to Frankfurt, Rome, then back to Lusaka. Thursday, the flight used to go to Bombay, and Friday, back to London. On Monday, the schedule would begin all over again.

One of the places we used to stay when we were traveling for Zambia Airways was the Intercontinental Hotel located right on top of Victoria Falls. The Vic Falls Hotel was like disembarking an airplane in the 1990s and stepping back in time to the 1930s. People actually pulled the fans by cords, and the white chalks were stones.

I remember enjoying sitting out on the veranda and drinking tea while overlooking the Falls.

But at night, when you were trying to sleep, the noise from the

Falls was deafening. Do you know what an underground train sounds like when you're standing above it? You heard this *boom, boom, boom, boom.* Victoria Falls was times that by five thousand percent!

When I started with Zambia Airways, their first widebody DC-10 had been in their fleet only a couple of months. Zambia Airways always had Boeing 707s, 737s, and British Aerospace BAe 748 tur-boprops to travel to destinations within the African continent. But the DC-10 was kingpin to the fleet, and the airplane needed to be on schedule. Every inbound passenger waited for that airplane.

If the DC-10 did not leave on time, all other departing flights within Africa would be late because all the baggage was sorted out for people staying in Lusaka or departures to other destinations inside Africa. Then those airplanes used to return and connect with the international flight to London. That was the same with the 707.

Remember that Zambia was a British colony. Back then, it was called Northern Rhodesia before it became Zambia. The airplanes were beautifully kept. The 707s were old at that stage, but they looked like they were brand new.

Zambia Airways was a focal point of national pride within the country. The airline was loved by the citizens and supported by the government.

If you gave passengers today the service that Zambia Airways gave back then, the airplanes would be full all the time because the service was fantastic compared to what you get now. The service was so outstanding that the airline won the best award during my tenure there.

Zambian cabin crew were trained by Swiss Air, an airline known for excellent cabin skills, quality and service. Swiss Air trained the native Zambian flight attendants, and they were so successful that Zambia Airways won an award for being the best airline in Africa. They were proud of the company. I think that was what I learned too. Through the excellence of their work, I could see a nation's pride.

During my time at Zambia Airways, I met Phil Battaglia, project pilot and test flight engineer for McDonnell Douglas on the Ultra High Bypass engine project at the time, who I came to call my "American Dad." Phil was the contract pilot for McDonnell Douglas when the DC-10 came online.

Since the DC-10 was brand new to Zambia, Phil was assigned to train the Zambian pilots and crew to fly and operate the plane and open up the new routes within the interior of Africa and intercontinental. Phil did all the check rides, simulations and ensured their knowledge and competency on the aircraft. He was McDonnell Douglas' representative for Zambia Airways with the singular mission of establishing the airplane on a national route. The DC-10 was christened *Nkwazi* — a Zulu word that means "fish eagle" and revered by many Zambian citizens.

The crews on the airline were a true melting pot, and Zambia Airways became one of the best loved airlines in Africa for what they did. The cockpit trained on 707s and the DC-10. The crew was always a true United Nations. Every time Phil got in the cockpit, there were people from different places. American, German, English, Portuguese, so many different nationalities.

Phil and I first met in London. He was a great guy and knew every-thing about aviation. Phil was an engineering test pilot, a lovely character, and a gentleman. We became close friends. When he was in London, I would take him around and show him the sights. We both saw possibilities, and sometimes, when you share your thoughts, you have what you need to move forward.

I had a vision of a charter air business for quite some time, and I was trying to establish my own charter company. Transcontinental Systems was my very first attempt to start my own business. I started thinking of an air charter business in Jersey, and the thought of it was never far from my mind the entire time I was with Zambia Airways until I came to America.

I was trying to get some various charters going and collect the different pieces together to make them fit. When I met the chief pilot and the chairman of Zambia Airways, Captain Godfrey, I asked, "Why aren't you guys using these planes for charters?" I saw tremendous possibilities, and we had a couple of requests, but Zambia Airways couldn't think outside the box. They regarded themselves as a scheduled airline only, and the idea of making money on charters was beyond their wave band thinking.

But I kept seeing chartering opportunities.

One day, we had a technical problem with the airplane, a DC-10 off in London, and it was the proverbial stormy night, complete with wind and rain.

They lost the pitot tube, which is an instrument located on both sides of the airplane. It is a tiny tube that sticks out and measures the airspeed of the plane. Without it, the captain and crew can't see how fast the airplane is going.

When the ground personnel pushed the jet bridge back for departure, the cords on the sides got caught around the pitot tube, dislodging the pitot tube from the side of the airplane as the plane pulled away from the jet bridge.

All of a sudden, you heard this ting-ting on the ground. I immediately said, "It sounds expensive."

Alitalia was our ground agent in London. They were great to work with, and we had a camaraderie that you can't explain. You just get it. I think camaraderie is intuitive in aviation in general, and maybe also in aerospace. In the best of worlds, everybody working together in harmony is the best you can have with any company.

We were sitting there, and our Alitalia engineer hurried back to his office to look for spare parts, whatever we needed. We had a full flight, and we needed to make an announcement to our passengers.

"Ladies and gentlemen, as you know, there's a windstorm. When we pushed back from the gate, the airplane sustained slight damage. Please bear with us while our ground agent assesses the situation and sees what needs to be done."

Parked next to the Zambian DC-10 was an Egypt Air A310 Airbus with the lights off and nobody on the plane. All set to go out the next morning.

All of a sudden, a lightning bolt hit me, and I thought, "Wouldn't it be nice if we knew that airplane had a crew, and we could use that airplane for this flight." It was as simple as that. That was how it all started. The thought of using the crew and planes that you have available.

That was not what happened that night.

Instead, there was a two-and-a-half-hour delay while we got the pitot tube fixed, and then we left. But the thought was there. The brainstorm of an initial thought process occurred to me that day.

I tried to do this with Transcontinental Systems, but it was the wrong time, wrong place.

It just wasn't in the cards. At that point, there was too much red tape in England, in Europe. I was too busy. I was flying. I was working at Zambia. I tried with Transcontinental Systems, but the penny hadn't dropped at this stage.

What I did recognize was that if I was really going to do this, I had to give it one hundred percent of my time. I couldn't have an airline job or be with an airline, or be doing something, anything else on the side as a safety net. I had to go all in.

Passion is the way forward.

CHAPTER 8

The America Dream

"I fly because it releases my mind from the tyranny of petty things." — Antoine de Saint-Exupery

A S THE CONTRACT WITH Zambia Airways began to wind down, I thought, "What's next?" I was getting itchy feet again. I was searching for the next stage of my life, and I had a clean sheet of paper in front of me.

I felt constrained in England, back to my trapped bird metaphor.

I felt a familiar oppression from the English weather in the winter, from sending airplanes off while trying to establish my dream of a charter business in England but getting stymied at every turn. I was finding the English way of life, the European way of life, limiting.

Every effort to launch Transcontinental Systems, my first charter business, seemed like taking three steps forward and two steps back. The progress was painfully slow. I was testing the structure of my charter concept with Transcontinental Systems, but there was so much red tape, so many administrative hurdles. Whenever I presented a new proposal in England, a corresponding regulation or governmental detail would not allow me to implement it. That created a negative atmosphere for me, and I wanted to escape that pessimism.

When my American Dad, Phil Battaglia, completed his training missions with the pilots of Zambia Airways, he returned to the United States. We stayed in touch, communicating back and forth. I would always ask him the same question, "Are there any possibilities for me at McDonnell Douglas?"

And Phil answered honestly, "That's really not your cup of tea. I don't see you doing that."

But America was on my mind. I always had a fascination about America. I first visited New York when working with El Al and stayed for a while on vacation.

All the American people I met over the years have been so friendly. I had childhood friends from Wheelus Air Force base in Libya that I played with while visiting my sister. I was quite close with Phil and other people in the aviation business. They were so different from Europeans. Americans appeared fresh. Open. I imagined the American lifestyle was like the Brady Bunch. It was an appealing draw.

Freedom is always enticing.

While working with Zambia Airways, our handling agent in London was Pan Am, an American airline. I was involved with American companies. I met other reps for McDonnell Douglas. They were great guys, innovative, and willing to challenge the limits of air travel. Just being involved with them, I realized that they were the future of aerospace.

McDonnell Douglas was leading aviation into actual space flight. They dreamed big. And with each American I met, I thought, "My God, these people are really good." And that was the first time that I started to understand the concept of the American Dream.

In England and Europe, Americans have a tarnished reputation of being brash and a bit loudmouth. But Americans are the melting pot, and that's just the way they communicate. Americans say what the British and other Europeans might be thinking, but don't say, and that's refreshing and exciting.

I don't think people who live in America see that openness or appreciate that freedom as much as they should. In fact, I'm so much American now that sometimes I have to take a step back and look down. I went to the beach with my wife the other day. We stood and looked around at the coast of California. Because we're lucky enough to see it all the time, maybe the scene doesn't resonate as clearly or as much as it once did.

But when you're from another country . . . For example, what if you live in Tahiti? Some people think Tahiti is penultimate great. But if you really look at some areas, it's not very nice. If you live there all the time, you don't realize what an incredibly beautiful place you're in. If you live in Scandinavia, you don't understand what a unique, special place it is.

Sometimes you have to go to other places to come back and appreciate the place you do live in. When anybody tells me they don't like America, I answer, "For all its dysfunction, Americans will get it right eventually." But if I were to take that person and put them in some of the places I've been, they'd be back here so quick their heads would fly off.

There is something about America that can't be done anywhere else on the planet. I think that a lot of people don't realize what an absolute pleasure it is to be here. If you're persistent and work hard in America, you can do it. You can make it happen.

And so, when the Zambia contract ended, and the big question was once again, "What do I do?"

I said to myself, "In for a penny, in for a pound. The only way you're going to do it, Tracey Deakin, is if you just do it."

I knew that I wanted to go to America. I didn't know why, but I knew. I've always known. I wanted to be in America. Always.

Experiences generate the spark. I think the decisions in my life were based on those experiences and Phil Battaglia, my American Dad, was the definite spark. Each one of the sparks you get in your life accumulates to create a big rocket going all the way up into outer space. The big thing is the journey up. You don't know the destination, but you get these little re-lights. Thanks to boosters now and again, the rocket pushes you up farther and farther until you eventually get to your destination.

In December 1987, I felt like the proverbial super comet as I boarded an airplane bound for the United States. I didn't stop to think about what it might take to make it happen. But I was determined to do it, and that was where the British bulldog in my personality comes in. I understood that the British bulldog must be tamed. He is best paired with a sheepdog because the sheepdog is very good at keeping sheep happy in her pen, but the British bulldog goes after any foxes or coyotes threatening the flock.

Believe it or not, I was on Pan Am 103, the same Pan Am 103 that was blown up in the Lockerbie tragedy almost exactly a year later on December 21, 1988. At the time, Pan Am 103 was a scheduled service that flew from London to Seattle and then Seattle to Los Angeles.

It was Christmas, and Phil graciously offered for the hospitality of his home.

But when I arrived in Los Angeles, my first impression was the smog. "What the hell is that smell?" I asked Phil.

He replied, "That's smog."

And I said, "That's totally disgusting."

Three days prior to Christmas, I drove down to Dana Point, a picture-perfect place here in California, with a lovely harbor filled with different types of boats. I remember sitting there and having a drink at sunset.

I opened a napkin and drew a line down the middle. On one side, I planned to write all my reasons for staying in America, and on the other side, all my reasons for going elsewhere.

But when I started writing, all I wrote was America, America, America, America.

So, I stayed with Phil in Huntington Beach for almost two months.

During the day, I visited all the FBOs of every single airport in Southern California. I saw everybody I could, asked questions, listened, and generally introduced myself to the aviation community.

One day, I was walking around the Long Beach airport, and as I went up the ramp, I bumped into Ken Haas of Alpha Jet. Ken was quite distinctive with his handlebar mustache. He was standing on the ramp, so we started talking, like you do in aviation.

Ken was kind of like the Walter Mitty of aviation, a person with a lot of aviation experience and tremendous flying abilities. After the Vietnam War, Ken operated a flight department, and that was where he met his partner, Tom Cepek. The government was giving people money to help them get started in a career, and many of them took the money and were learning to fly. Ken Haas taught them how to fly Learjets way before I knew him.

Ken managed Tom's airplane, a Learjet 25, and kept it at his hangar in Long Beach. There was nothing else in that 220,000 square foot hangar. The space was huge, and it was empty except for that single Learjet. The aircraft looked like a bumblebee in the back of the hangar! A tiny, little thing!

As we stood together talking on the ramp, I asked Ken what he was doing. He replied, "Well, I've got this facility, and we're starting a company called Alpha Jet."

Then I told him about my experience with aviation and charters. I finally broached the subject, and said, "Actually, I'm just out here looking, between you and me."

He said, "What's your status here?"

I said, "Status, what do you mean?"

He asked, "Are you a resident, or what are you?"

I said, "I'm just here." I didn't want to advertise that at the time, I was an illegal alien. However, I did become a US citizen several years later.

He said, "Well, if you'd like to have a job, let's try it out together."

So, I started work for him the following Monday morning. I think I worked there for almost three months without getting paid anything. He was taking advantage of me. I understood that. But he was also taking a risk on me, and I was giving him a trial run, but it ended up being a very good relationship.

CHAPTER 9

Flying the Socks Off

"Pilots are a rare kind of human. They leave the ordinary surface of the world, to purify their soul in the sky, and they come down to earth, only after receiving the communion of the infinite." — Jose Maria Velasco Ibarra

I N THAT SHORT AMOUNT of time, three bare months, we got the Long Beach Jet Center, which became a very formidable FBO, up and running.

I was on my way. Tracey Deakin was doing what he loved and wanted to do because he knew his stuff. He had a charter company going. He was making it happen.

Later, I met Ken's partner, Tom, the owner of the single Learjet in the hangar. We started with charters on that one aircraft. Then everything started to come together because I began to outreach, and nobody was doing that. This was where my earlier experience came in. This really wasn't standard operating procedure here in the United States, so it was out of their comfort zone. They didn't know how to organize and execute a charter business. So not only were we flying the socks off the planes that we had in-house, but we were also flying the socks off other people's airplanes.

Within eight or nine months, we had all types of airplanes in the hangar. Executive aircraft like Learjet, Cessna, Gulfstream, and the famous Lockheed TriStar. We had VIP passes, and our lounge was well-appointed and immaculate.

I would walk up and down the hangar floor with one of these commercial mops to keep it spotless. There were certain times of day when the hangar doors were open that I would have to wear a pair of sunglasses because the reflection of the sun off the floor was so powerful.

One afternoon, Marrten Kylstra, who eventually was Best Man for my wedding, and I were just about ready to head out the door for a bite to eat when, yet another Gulfstream appeared around the corner.

Maarten stopped and listened. "I think it's coming to us," he said.

"Yeah, coming to us," I agreed, and we were both stunned because nobody had told us anything. Usually, a company's chief pilot would come out and visit FBOs before any planes showed up. IBM had come out to see us recently, but they hadn't told us that we were awarded their contract.

So, the airplane pulled in, and we had just finished servicing that one when another plane rounded the corner.

What was going on?

By the end of the evening, Maarten and I had serviced five aircraft. Where they all came from, we didn't have a clue.

I can still remember our first Boeing 727. If it hadn't had been for my experience, I wouldn't have known how to deal with those. Airliners started to come to us. When we didn't have enough ramp space, we would taxi the airplane into the hangar and shut it up. People were amazed. We would taxi the plane all the way to the hangar, then open the doors. Inside, we had all the buses and everything else you needed there, waiting for them.

The flight crews were amazed at our efficiency.

I would smile and say, "Please come into the hangar."

Then everybody and anybody, including the mechanics, came out to help unload and load airplanes and do anything else necessary to help and support. It was essential to get everybody going. All hands-on deck!

We booked charters all over the place. Initially, most of our work was for the airlines, but then as I gradually started collecting more and more contacts, satisfied customers would recommend us. Finally, potential customers would just call us up and say they heard about us through referrals. So, I was running the FBO, as well as doing Alpha Jet.

I wore a lot of different hats.

I contacted all my early airline customers, people that I had known for years. One of our first major clients was Flying Tigers, now part of FedEx. I offered charters for one of the ex-owners of Flying Tigers. We would do between five and seven flights a week for them. We could have an airplane ready to go on charter within forty-five minutes or less, usually about twenty minutes on average. They used to call us up and say they needed to move a part or something else as soon as possible. Give us a quote! Boom, I gave the quote. Yep, we're doing it.

Two essential pieces of equipment were my pager and my bike. Some days I had to use the bike to find the payphone. I would call the pilot or co-pilot. Sometimes, they were speaking to their girlfriend or their wife, so I would say, "operator, emergency connect." And the operator used to emergency connect with them while they were speaking. I'd interrupt and say, "I need you to get up here now. You're going to Reno or to San Francisco or Portland."

Within fifteen to twenty minutes, the co-pilot filed all our flight plans. If I was at our facility, I would help with the aircraft departure prep and walk around prior to the crew arrival. Maarten would tip the fuel full or refuel if necessary. The captain and the crews could get in, jump off and go. Nobody could match us, so we built our reputation and business with all the airlines through my contacts. From that, corporate clients began to appear from word-of-mouth referrals. Customers would call or come by and say they heard about this "English guy."

You know, aviation is very campy, very flaky in some respects. Still, it's nice to know that, when requested, my clients knew I would deliver. Every single time I would deliver their something somewhere, and even if it didn't go according to plan all the time, I would get it done.

Various corporate flight departments such as Toyota and local hospitals and even the national human organ transplant centers began to hear about us. They knew when they spoke to me that this was not only about a charter, but also about safety and performance.

Our reputation was built on our standards. And that was when I started to look at these other companies and ask hard questions about safety, insurance, pilot training, and maintenance. What was being done correctly? What was not?

When I first arrived in the United States and went to work for Alpha Jet, we had our own airplanes. When we couldn't use our own planes, I used to go out to find what our client needed. Also, people who owned airplanes came to me because they knew about our work. They would ask, "Can you help out with this?"

At that point, when I began to procure airplanes from other people to use for charter work, I realized that there were very few standards present in the industry. Air charter work was a new idea that developed over time.

At first, I thought clients looking for a charter flight, and those who owned underutilized aircraft, looked me up because they knew I was reliable. I would make sure they received the service they required for the mission that was in front of them. I was careful to listen to their needs and then locate the airplane that could do the job. It began to occur to me that there were a myriad of possibilities relating to available service, pricing, and standards applied to the aircraft and the crews that wanted the job.

I share an example about a group of crew members that turned up for an executive flight dressed in shorts. I was like, "Hang on, go away." Then, another time an airplane arrived nice enough on the outside, but nothing in the interior matched up.

I recognized the need for some internal policing.

Obviously, I needed to prepare for the worst, and to review and consider a boatload of information. But in my mind, I wondered that if the crew and the interior of the plane were so lax, then how meticulous were the safety checks, engine maintenance, and training requirements of the aircraft?

Kenny and I worked really well together. We started the FBO.

When you opened the door of the hangar, the floor was gray concrete, and it was always immaculate. Our lounge had plush carpets, nice sofas. We had employees that were courteous and attentive. The operation was nice and comfortable, and we were making money from charters.

But later, in our time together, it was Ken who got the itchy feet. He wanted to fly for the airlines, and he went back to work for MGM.

When I flew with Ken Haas, he was a total ambassador of aviation, just like Phil Battaglia. When these men got in the cockpit, something was calming about them, something knowledgeable. They had a sixth sense. I've only picked up on that a few times in my life, and it was a privilege to know both of those gentlemen.

I salute them.

But I could see Ken was divided. He wanted to fly, but he also enjoyed the company, and he couldn't do both at the same time. Also, I had already learned some things that seemed to be lost on him.

I was running the FBO, as well as Alpha Jet. He left me with responsibility for the whole thing, and I began to chafe. I didn't think that was right.

Ken had an accountant, a financial CFO that took care of the money. But when the airplanes taxied in, I made all the decisions and did all the work. Absolutely! Bring it on in! People couldn't believe the number of aircraft coming into our facility. I remember the first time we had a 727-executive airplane in there, a giant plane. No one could quite believe it.

But I also remember one flight I took up to San Francisco with Ken. He could tell I was not happy, and I told him I was not. I was managing all the details and not really being rewarded for it. So, I told him, and that was why I ultimately left.

He asked, "What can I do?"

And I tried to explain. Maybe I didn't verbalize enough. I probably hadn't got it together in my own mind at that stage. I was in my early thirties. I expressed my frustration with the situation. I felt we weren't going anywhere. No changes were being made. He actually said to me at dinner, "I've never met anybody like you, ever. There is no question. You are going to go a long way in aviation."

Prior to knowing Ken, he and Tom were in an airplane accident. They were flying around in a Pitts Special, which is an aerobatic airplane. Apparently, on the way back to Long Beach, they crashed beside the runway. Both men got out, but Ken had something wrong with his stomach. Whatever medical problem he was grappling with didn't quite recover, and later, he had to return to hospital. While he was there, he had a fatal heart attack.

CHAPTER 10

California Epicenter

"Sometimes, flying feels too God-like to be attained by man. Sometimes, the world from above seems too beautiful, too wonderful, too distant for human eyes to see."

— Charles A. Lindbergh

A FTER I LEFT ALPHA Jet, I worked a short stint with Universal Weather and Aviation in Texas. The company wanted me to move down to Houston, but I felt like I'd just arrived in California, and I had only recently purchased a house.

What hit me was I had been living out of a suitcase since I left my parent's home until that point. I'd been moving all over the place for years. I felt like I had finally landed, and I wanted to be on the ground for a while.

I worked in Houston during the week and traveled back every weekend to my house in California and then flew out Sunday night. But I was tired of the constant motion, and I just couldn't bring myself to live in Texas. No disrespect to Texans, but it was not my cup of tea.

Universal Weather and Aviation was very accommodating, to the point of opening up an office in Long Beach for a while. They made every effort to keep me, but I just didn't like the structure. While I was in that office, they wanted me to speak to the clients I had at Alpha Jet, but they weren't allowing me to do anything with them. People were calling me up wanting charters, and Universal wouldn't allow me to book any charters with them. Then, they kept pushing me to move to Texas. I didn't feel comfortable about it, and soon, we came to a parting of ways. I was done with it.

About that time, I met Peter Le Bas, who owned and managed Le Bas Limousines. I was referred to Peter by Don Kirk, a friend of mine who lived in Dana Point. He had talked about Peter's limousine company, and I was actually looking for a reliable limousine company. But, unfortunately, many limo companies at the time tended to show up late or just not show up at all.

Don said, "There's this Irish guy I know, and he's in Seal Beach." And I said, "Sure, I'll talk to him."

We met there, after which I began to use his limo service. I was impressed. He managed the company professionally, and the service was reliable. Couldn't ask for more.

Peter and I became good friends. I then met the person who eventually became our third partner, Patrick Hampton. Peter and Patrick were boyhood friends. They've known each other for years and used to race motorbikes together. We used to meet up for drinks and come over to my house or his house to talk and brainstorm about starting a business.

Finally, I called Peter, who was in Ireland. I said, "How about this idea? Maybe we should do something together. You've got a limousine company. Why don't I get airplanes going? I'll do the aviation side of the company. We'll do it that way."

That was how we got going. I had all my contacts, and I felt the idea was a natural.

When Peter came back from Ireland, we sat on his steps, opened a beer, and talked more about it. I had known Peter for about two years at this point. I said, "Yeah, what do you think?" I related my experience with Transcontinental Systems, trying to get it all started. And then I thought, "Well, hang on a second. Limousines. I always have problems with limousines. Get rid of that side of things. Airplanes. I do the airplanes; Peter does the limousines."

Patrick and Peter were starting Le Bas International, but it hadn't even started at that stage. It was just about to launch. Peter had a local limousine company in Seal Beach. Patrick was working for Brendan Tours, a tour operator. I suggested, "Why don't we get airplanes involved?"

Each of us brought our own expertise, a unique *"je ne sais quoi"* to the enterprise. I was the only one with aviation expertise, and I had years of contacts to share. Patrick was great with computers and all types of technical wizardry. He took care of all the computer stuff. He was also very adept at accounting and legal, crossing the T's and dotting the I's.

Peter had his knowledge of people, his entertainment connections, and limousine business savvy. Years ago, he worked for his brother selling musical instruments. As he went out to the public to sell these musical instruments, he acquired a certain amount of street smarts and was very entrepreneurial.

I came from the tailoring business and owed so much to my father for his customer-centric approach and consideration of detail.

We combined those skill sets into a toolbox that has served us well.

We all brought something to the table. We pooled our expertise, and as I've said, information shared is powerful. When push comes to shove, all three of us find a solution.

That has been why our company has not only survived but thrived. We will get to the bottom of a problem and handle it, always have done. And that says a lot. We each put $7,500 into Le Bas International to get it going. We've been in business since 1990 and are now a billion-dollar company. That is quite a value on return.

The only other question was what to call the company.

Peter asked me, "What do you want to call it? Do you mind calling it Le Bas International? We'll call it air division." The limousine went years ago, and all I cared about was getting the enterprise off the ground. Today, if you ask around in the world, what Le Bas International means, no one knows it's somebody's last name. In some ways, the name is good because it is a complicated name to say. So, it sticks out once you get it in your head.

Le Bas International's first office was in a converted church in Seal Beach. My goodness, gracious, there was some language in that church back then. The limousine business was in the front, and the air division was in the back office.

Later, we made a whole new back office for the air division. We had maps around the walls and plotting charts up for the airplane charters. We had an extensive computer system in the back. Patrick built that and even put all the cabinets up. So that was where we first started. And we all took the money we made and invested it back in the company.

Patrick set up a computer. I put all my knowledge, everything I had, into that computer, especially how to search for available aircraft. Then, we began to write our operating manual, the protocols of our business that are still in place and still adhered to by our employees.

In the early days of Le Bas International, it was me doing all the charters, doing all of it. As I started to train Peter and Patrick, they quickly learned what and how I was operating, and twenty-four hours a day, we used to rotate the bag phone. We took it home with us if we were on call, and they learned from me. Every third night, you'd be on the night, handling anything that came in from our European clients.

Because of all the business that we generated out of Europe, we took the next logical step and opened our European office. We were the very first air charter company to do that.

So, twenty-four hours a day, every day of the week, if you call our office, the phone is answered within three rings, and a real person is on the phone who is knowledgeable and ready to speak with you. No one had ever done that before on a global level.

Since Peter and Patrick are both Irish, opening our second office in Shannon, Ireland, made sense. Peter pitched the idea, and I said, "Okay, let's try it." So that was what we did, and we're still doing it now. And it works. With two offices, we cover the globe in real-time in two twelve-hour shifts.

We've looked at the possibility of opening an office in Australia or New Zealand, or Singapore, so we could go to three eight-hour shifts. But the most significant driving power in our business, in aviation, is the United States, followed by Europe, followed by South America. So that's where our time and attention are focused . . . And business is picking up.

Asia is massive, but it's not yet as developed because of cultural differences. It's tough to get into China and a challenge to get permits to fly over Asian countries. In Europe or America, or even South America, it's relatively easy to get in there once you apply for the traffic landing permits. In Asian countries, it may take up to three weeks to gain access. You can't just go in the next day.

In retrospect, when I think about forming a company, I think of the ideas and concepts we are now implementing that we possibly should have implemented years ago. So, yes, you can always look through the looking glass and say we should have done this or that.

But again, on the other side of things, the world has changed, aviation has evolved. Now I think, "As long as you've done it. That's what's important."

In October 2020, we celebrated our third decade. As my partner, Peter, says, "How many marriages last that long?" Three decades in business is a huge accomplishment!

Our success stems from a lot of different areas. From the beginning, we have had several goals. We want to be engaged with the clients. We don't want to be snobby. There's a lot of Britishness, I suppose, in our approach. Snappy little things that we say in our conversations that aspire to the client. You can be a stiff concierge desk with your nose in the air. Or you can be at the bottom end. But we want to be between the middle and the upper crust. We aim to provide excellent service, but with sincere friendliness about it.

Have a good laugh about it along the way. That's what we try for. We deliver our services in a friendly, open way that the clients understand and appreciate.

Global Reach. Personal Touch™.

That's our motto. The principle of personal touch came from me because of my background in customer service. That's what we want to deliver globally. No matter where you are, you're an individual. Everybody, it doesn't matter who you are on the airplanes; you're all distinct, separate people.

How long did it take us to get the company organized and going?

Day one. Because of my contacts and references, we had clientele pretty much straight away.

The very first client request for charter flights was from In-N-Out Burger. The first flight was for Airborne Express, an overnight carrier, which was in a Citation I on 11/10/1990 with our reference number 5468 Alpha. We flew a spare part for an airplane from Long Beach up to Oakland.

Our first big celebrity booking was the Pink Floyd world tour. It came about via a gentleman that used to be with Air London who left to start his own company. We were doing other business with him. He said, "I've got this tour coming up for Pink Floyd over in the States. Can you help out?" So, we sourced the airplane for the band, the singers, the technicians, the setup team.

Global Reach. Personal Touch. There's me, Peter, and Patrick. Peter goes out on flights, reps' flights with top-end clients, and makes sure everything's going well. Patrick does all the computer and accounting stuff. That's his job. I'm the one who is good at interacting with clients and handling the logistics of the assignment. That's my job. Our mission, every day of our over thirty years, is to remain committed to the goal.

CHAPTER 11

Safety First

"Flying isn't dangerous. Crashing is what's dangerous."
— Unknown

F ROM THE VERY BEGINNING of Le Bas International, we
established three fundamental anchors. Safety is first, without a
doubt. Personal Touch, excellence in customer service, is second.
And privacy is third. All these touchstones come from three different
angles or perspectives, but safety is always number one.

What exactly do I mean by safety? Am I referring to the mechanics
of the aircraft? The pilot? The crew?

I'm talking about the whole package.

As far back as 1988, I began studying the differentials between
one crew member and others in the same crew, the type of airplane,
the cost, and every additional variable that I considered important
and worthy of examination.

At the time, there was no objective standard of safety other than
surviving take-off and landing, which is still supreme. But starting
then and expanding from my global experience, I began to center my
knowledge of safety and focus on examining various factors contributing
to best practices.

First, I implemented my early ideas that I had while still working
at Alpha Jet. And then, I began to get calls from the flight departments
of different airlines. Even people who had private airplanes would
contact me about my thoughts on the subject.

I documented my observations and conclusions. In fact, I had a physical black book where I downloaded all the experience from my brain and entered the results of all my findings on companies that I had conducted due diligence on.

Eventually, everything was transferred to computers, but I took that black book and the methods of investigation with me when I started Le Bas International with my two partners.

How did I approach the task of due diligence?

When speaking with a company that I had experience with and was already actively using, I would ask, "Who do you know in this area that is good?"

We called this our "Star Trek First Contact."

If I got three different referrals from First Contacts on one company, then I would speak to them.

When I interviewed the new company, I asked about their crews, how they found crews, their experience, and what they did to maintain current training. From there, I would start to get an idea of who they were and how they operated long before I considered introducing them to our clients and putting them in the airplanes.

My book of information grew and finally extended to every destination on the globe where I knew we had a vendor. If I needed somebody in Memphis or Florida, I would already have the names of contacts, their telephone numbers, what airplanes and/or crew they had.

In the early days of Le Bas, if someone needed an airplane, I used to put their requirements into what would almost be unrecognizable as a computer today. The machine had a flat screen, a handle, and a floppy disk. But I would put the request in there and run it against little codes that I knew from flying airplanes and had programmed into the computer to act like search engines. I'd put in the mission parameters, and all these names used to pop up. I would then call up vendors for possible availability, based on my research.

But at that point, the vetting process for the vendors was thorough and already complete. I wasn't scrambling. I was assured that I had done my homework ahead of time to ensure that the choice met the criteria and was as safe as possible.

In the United States, the FAA and the Civil Aviation Authorities' job is to make sure that specific safety standards have been met before the public boards an aircraft. They dictate the minimum requirements an airplane must maintain to allow passengers in the air. An aircraft must be safe; it's got to have the bolts on and pass testing criteria.

But at that time, when it came to customer service, there were no agreed upon standards.

The lack of an established benchmark relates to risk because a client may approach me and say, "Can you do this, can you do that?" Many people are willing to push the envelope, meaning the risk level, beyond what they should do just to get the job. Or they don't provide what they promised. Or they flat out lie and say something can be done when it can't.

Very early on, I recognized a real need for checks and balances in our customer service principles.

The most important thing about flight safety today is pilot training. Because pilots are the necessary mainstay, today the Federal Aviation Administration (FAA), requires 1,500 hours to fly as a commercial airline pilot.

I remember speaking to Lee Crowley, the chief pilot of Nike. He was a British guy who was really pleasant and possessed incredible knowledge about customer safety and service standards. A wonderful gentleman. Lee used to be in the marine business before moving to aviation. Absolutely looked a bit like David Niven, just like my father. I mean, he did. He was very well-spoken, had a little mustache. I can still see him now. Absolute pleasure to work with. Whatever you asked him to do, it was going to happen. He was that type of character.

The first time I ever met with him was in the early '90s. He was bringing Phil Knight, or somebody, down to Los Angeles. So, he drove up to our office in Seal Beach at the time,, and we went to breakfast. I was busy doing something typical Tracey, half forgetting

I raced over to meet Lee for breakfast, and then when I went to pay, I realized that I had forgotten my wallet.

I said, "I'll leap back and get it." And he said, "No, don't worry about it." So, it became a running joke between us, "Have you brought your wallet this time?" But that's what makes friendships.

We became good friends, and we both unequivocally agreed that standards for customer safety and service came down to pilot training and insurance.

We often talked over breakfast about this. As a result, Lee kindly introduced me to Nike's insurance broker, and Izzy Bowen, in charge Air Security, who was not only top-notch but, like me, had worked with Israeli Airlines. I'm always glad to start on common ground. Aviation tends to be a big wide circle in a small world.

I was interested in learning anything I could on the subject. When it came to insurance, I asked Lee to refer me to his aviation insurance broker for advice. I immediately went to her and asked point-blank, "How does the insurance industry look at risk?"

She replied with a wealth of information which boiled down to the following statement: "Well, it's the pilot. Or the pilots and their operations, but it's mostly the pilot and their training."

So, that was where we started, and we expanded on that. But, still, the original idea born of our early morning discussions was that training hours equals safety, and safety equals better insurance rates. So, in other words, the insurance company will not issue insurance to you if they think you're going to be a problem, if you're going to be a risk.

I continued to talk to both of them, and then I also went to the National Business Aircraft Association trade shows to speak directly to insurance brokers at the event.

From that base, my brain assimilated a framework for what risk meant to the client and what risk looked like in the aviation world. In other words, you have a pilot who can fly a 747, but maybe he just has a private pilot's license. He can fly it. He's checked out on it, but perhaps he doesn't have the number of hours necessary to check out on it for commercial purposes. What did that look like at the top end?

We started to research then recommend minimum hours of pilot time that the insurance company would accept as a margin for safety. The result was that we more often sought vendors where the pilots met these standards to fly safely.

The more hours a pilot has on a type of airplane, the less risk, and risk translates into dollars.

The insurance company used to assign dollars for the prospective aviation company based on the risk of pilots. With all that information, we formed a framework of what the risk factors might look like. But we also realized that we had to consider other factors. We focused on the debate and discovered what now appears obvious.

Generally, if a company has good insurance, then most likely it's a decent company. If the company is well-backed financially, they will probably have proper maintenance. Whether they have a sound accounting system that pays their people fairly and on time seems to make a difference. All of this needs to be continuously checked.

The various factors that we studied started to evolve faster and gel into a complete picture of what necessary fundamentals might look like in the safety world. At the same time, we also had to be conscious of our discussions at the NBAA with the insurance brokers. If you over-asked or overstated essentials, then you were never going to get anybody to fly because they couldn't afford it.

There is always a balancing act.

If you wanted insurance back then of $300 million, most companies wouldn't have the money to afford that level. Perhaps if they were a big company that had quite a few airplanes, then it might be possible. But at what point did the balance tip (and go beyond the purpose of safety) to where the cost of the insurance was just not feasible in the real world?

From that starting point, we developed the Air Carrier's Commercial Operating Manual (ACCOM), a classification not only based on information that was coming from insurance companies but also from actual people, professional pilots, flight departments, and airlines. We wrote our own flight safety manual to implement the checks and balances based on our findings.

In other words, we adopted the "First Contact" method. We would reach out to vendors that we didn't know but were suggested as possible associates for us. For example, another vendor might recommend a new company X. If we heard that company X's name mentioned three times in conversation, we would then think, "Okay, it may be worth our time to speak with them."

We would then contact the possible vendor X and query them about the insurance they had in place, how much, etc. Primarily, however, we would ask about their pilots.

That is our standard operating procedure now.

For every flight, we require a certain level of insurance. We also have standards for time of pilot training and hours, both time and type, on each particular aircraft.

If vendor X doesn't meet those standards, we cannot use its airplane. I won't say that when we apply those standards, we'll never get into trouble. There's always going to be the "what if?" lurking in the background when it comes to flying but adhering to tested established policies keeps us as close as humanly possible to staying out of trouble and providing the best possible safety to our clients.

So, that was where our customer service and safety standards all came from.

I can remember Peter and myself walking around the NBAA trade show, and we saw this company called Wyvern that claimed to be involved with flight standards. "Ooh, who's this?" we wondered.

We went up and spoke to them, and I had a bit of trouble with their approach. This was long before Air Carriers Association of North America (ACANA) existed, and I couldn't quite square it in my brain.

I had problems with Wyvern because it was an audit company. They wanted to do audits on flight departments for flight safety and for charter companies, which I thought was basically a good idea. But on the other side of my brain, I was thinking, "Hang on. Isn't that what civil aviation authorities are meant to do around the globe? That's their job." We talked about it. At first, they were a bit, for a better word, snobbish. At the time, we were in that envelope where brokers were looked down upon. So, they looked down upon us because we weren't an operator. They didn't know that we had done all this work on flight safety.

A couple of years later, a charming gentleman, Jim Betlyon, purchased Wyvern, and he got me on the phone because he had heard about us and what we were doing. He couldn't understand why I wouldn't join Wyvern. I simply said, "Because we have our own flight standards." So, he flew out to meet with us. He came into my office, and I showed him our flight standards. He immediately said, "I understand now why you don't use us."

But I began to speak to Jim more and more over time about the flight safety standard issues that concerned me, and eventually, we agreed to assimilate our stuff into his.

The best practices we developed became part of Wyvern, an organization that monitors and audits aviation safety and risk management standards.

In my initial discussion with Lee, the Nike pilot, we shared information, but we didn't manage airlines. We were not a flight safety department. Wyvern is the organization that makes the inspections to determine whether these standards are met. Let them do it, as long as it's done, and it is done.

Le Bas International is a Wyvern-approved broker. Not everyone is.

For a brief time, we had our own Irish Operating Certificate, AOC in 1996. At Alpha Jet, we were pure charter. But as we developed Le Bas and grew to where we are now, we evolved into a pure brokerage company. Yes, we were often regarded with disrespect by a lot of people who had their own airplanes. Their perception was that the charter companies or charter people were taking the business away from them.

They weren't really seeing the big picture, or perhaps the big picture has moved with the times. Today, the charter business has progressed.

Most of the companies out there are not charter companies but management companies. They manage these airplanes. And so, it's kind of like leasing a car. They take care of the aircraft. They water it, oil it, electrify it and provide a driver and crew.

In the early days, these companies made a lot of revenue from charters, mainly because tax write-offs were lucrative. Initially, they thought their business was being pulled away by brokers. They didn't see the big picture. They didn't understand that a brokerage company like ours is an arm of a professional organization with global clients.

We bring those global clients to the table. If you consider all the very top-end professional brokers in today's world, and put them together, we would probably be as big (or bigger) than some of the largest airlines on the planet.

The amount of business that we control is massive.

But back in the day, the charter companies didn't appreciate that concept. We encountered a lot of the pushback from them, and not only about flight safety. I concede that there will always be some unscrupulous people running questionable companies within any industry. They are the kind that won't follow standards and only look at the bottom line.

There's a concept being touted out there nowadays called "seat-sharing" that I believe is a bit dubious. The seat-sharing companies are doing it all wrong, and I fear the result will be an accident.

Flight safety is the ultimate example of the necessity of sheepdogging.

You can never let safety out of the bag, and many good people are committed to best practices. Regrettably, others get sucked in because they see big money, glitter, or entertainers. People in our industry have gone to jail . . . a lot of them for corruption.

That's the purpose of the organization focused on safety standards that we've brought to the table. To police the industry and firmly state that bad behavior is not acceptable. I sincerely wish that we all care about getting our passengers or cargo from point A to point B safely and efficiently. That we do what we're meant to do. On-time.

So, to backtrack, my work with flight safety is ongoing. Le Bas International has supported my efforts, and we are an approved broker, one of the founding members of the Air Carriers Association of North America (ACANA). We banded together with other like-minded companies in the same hemisphere because we are dedicated to the best in customer aviation safety. We support and adhere to flight safety standards.

I've contacted a host of people and related organizations to bring them into ACANA: Paul McCloskey, David McCowan, companies like Hunt & Palmer, Chapman, Freeborn, and Air Partner. I've known Air Partner since they were Air London, the original company founded sixty years ago. Now, they're one of the biggest charter brokers on the planet. So, I reached out to these people to bring them into the ACANA organization.

In 1998, Le Bas had its own Crystal Globe Award, an honor that recognizes operators that best meet the organization's flight safety standards. Again, this was way ahead of everyone else.

Currently, two organizations, Wyvern and ARGUS, exist to conduct inspections on air charter companies. In fact, the general public won't fly on a charter airplane now if it doesn't have a rating from one of these two companies. Wyvern and ARGUS do not yet have a global presence but operate primarily in the United States and Europe.

In other parts of the world, we still backfill and do the work ourselves to ensure our customer safety standards are upheld on every aircraft we charter, just like we did years ago. If I'm selecting an airplane out of Australia or out of Africa, we still adhere to the protocol and apply our best practices standards on a global scale. Before every single flight that we offer, we do a check. And if that check is not done or the criteria are not met, an offer is not made.

Many charter operators worldwide have developed a perceived bias against air charter brokers, and eventually they demanded that the US Department of Transportation (DOT) step in and examine brokers under a microscope.

When the DOT came to ACANA to research and investigate, we'd already done the work. Much of the information that we organized and presented to them is now codified into a law as 14 CFR Part 295 (effective as of February 14, 2019).

That was a long time coming. I had worked on that for years and years.

As the Le Bas International website states: "On February 14, 2019, the Department of Transportation (DOT) recognized Air Charter Brokers for the first time, publishing new regulations, 14 Code of Federal Regulations (CFR) Part 295, Air Charter Brokers, and revising regulations 14 CFR Part 298, Exemptions for Air Taxi and Commuter Air Carrier Operations.

A large part of the regulatory change is mandating the full disclosure to customers of a Broker's relationships with Part 135 and 121 operators on contracts, websites, and other marketing materials. That includes letting customers know a Broker is only arranging, not operating, a charter flight."

We're proud to have been part of the movement that contributed to the passage of this regulation. I am pleased to have supported the definition and implementation of passenger safety standards. For three decades, we operated transparently, and met the criteria of the new regulations long before the process to regulate our industry even began.

Years ago, the air charter industry, which we participate in as brokers, never used to talk to each other. Then, David McCowen, currently President of the Americas or Chapman Freeborn, various other people and myself got together and started a continuing dialogue about best practices.

ACANA's purpose is to educate the public. If you're chartering an airplane, and if you follow ACANA's recommendations, you're going to keep yourself pretty safe.

Our next step will be to develop a database for aviation professionals and customers who use broker companies, so that if you have a question, you can find an answer. The biggest brokers on the planet want to share their knowledge of the industry. We're taking all that information and putting it where someone can quickly go and find the answers to their questions: "Okay, that's what to do. That's what to look for." And that's what the new ruling that became the law attempted as well.

Other organizations now exist, such as the Flight Safety Foundation and Air Safety Institute in Frederick, MD. Different ratings have begun to appear, which is fantastic because accidents have declined. Captain Sully Sullenberger, an aviation ambassador and United States Permanent Representative to the International Civil Aviation Organization and *Time's* Top 100 Most Inferential Heroes and Icons of 2009, speaks passionately on the subject.

An accident should be a rare occurrence in this day and age.

There will still be issues that crop up. Situations that go wrong, or conditions that flip upside down. But our industry has come a very long way. Does it need more work? Absolutely. But that is where we've gotten to so far.

The goal is to learn from every accident and avoid it in the future. However, if another accident happens because of something that could have been changed or corrected, that is unforgivable.

CHAPTER 12

The Leopard's Claw

"What is the similarity between air traffic controllers and pilots? If a pilot screws up, the pilot dies; If ATC screws up, the pilot dies." — Unknown

AIRPLANES ARE EXQUISITE AND extraordinary, but the trouble is that they can be unpredictable, and that is usually attributed to mechanical issues, human beings, and weather. Remember the leopard's claw...

December 17, 1993. There have been a lot of moments as well as a lot of drama in my life and in my business. However, the biggest one, the one that still plagues me today, was the accident. This was my true motivation for exploring and expanding the standards of flight safety. The accident became my furnace for all the future work I just detailed on flight safety.

Harry and Esther Snyder founded In-N-Out Burger in Baldwin Park, CA, in 1948. It's an established and successful company. When I was with Alpha Jet, I got to know their son, Rich, quite well. Rich looked like Father Christmas. He was quite a large gentleman with a big rosy face.

Rich was such a lovely gentleman. And the company is warm, caring. If every corporation could be like In-N-Out Burger, the world would be a fantastic place. It's a brilliant organization, and I have frequently looked to their business model in our own enterprise. They're just so nice.

In-N-Out Burger was my first ever charter customer in the United States.

When we first got Le Bas going, we used to fly Rich around to different places in a Beechcraft King Air. Rich liked this one particular King Air that we used all the time along with the owner's private corporate pilot, John Hemingway.

I was always very conscious of safety. Obsessively so. Before I put clients on airplanes, I used to go out, look at them, and run a physical check. When Rich used a helicopter to travel to the Baldwin Park offices, I would go up there to martial helicoptering on the ramp. I would walk around the entire space to make sure there was no foreign object debris (FOD), no object that could fly up and hit the helicopter.

One afternoon, I remember going out to UPS, with whom we also used to do a lot of work for. On the way back, I went straight by the corporate office of In-N-Out Burger in Baldwin Park. The building looked like something out of Gone with the Wind.

As you opened the door, the reception area resembled a hotel check-in, and they had a giant sweeping staircase going all the way up to the second floor. Atop, there were banisters. I went in and said, "By chance, is Rich in today?" And I heard Rich answer, "Who's calling?"

I said, "Oh, it's Tracey, he knows me, and I just popped in . . ."

As I was saying it, Rich looked over the top of the balcony and said, "Tracey, where have you been? Don't you go anywhere."

Turned out, he had been thinking of a request he wanted to make. He said, "Tracey, I want to use one of these Israeli aircraft, the Westwind. Do you happen to know any?"

"Well," I said, "I do, but let me go and do some research."

And so, I did. That type of airplane and the actual pilots we used were very experienced. In fact, John Hemingway went for a check ride in the Westwind the day before the accident.

Anyway, the airplane was owned by the chairman of Anthem and maintained perfectly.

But on that day, Rich had made a store visit, and the aircraft was on the return leg of the fact-finding trip. His mother was on the flight, as well. When she traveled with Rich, we usually used to drop her off at Brackett Field, which is right near Baldwin Park. Afterwards, we would fly from there down to Orange County near where Rich lived right on the beach.

The airplane took off. It was a very short flight, like fifteen minutes. And it was descending, on its approach, coming into Orange County. The evening was beautiful, clear, typical California with no wind, just perfect.

I remember that I was in our office, just checking on things, making sure everything was good since I was on personal duty that night. I went home at 4:00 to get ready to take any phone calls.

While the Westwind was descending, a commercial flight (a United 757) was coming across at the same time over Seal Beach, and it was pretty high. The air traffic controller directed United, Flight Number 103, to land on runway 19 before the Westwind. Because of the entry from the downwind to the final on the visual 19 approach, the 757 was flying a nearly 6-degree glideslope. The Westwind, however, was tracking the Instrument Landing System — ILS on a normal 3-degree glideslope and closing in on the 757.

As the Westwind slowed to let United 757 go in first, the aircraft was caught by the larger plane's wake turbulence which is the disturbance that occurs behind a plane as it passes through the atmosphere.

The larger plane's wake turbulence caught the Westwind, flipped it upside down, and put it into a nosedive straight into the ground.

I was at home when I got a call from Peter, who said, "There might have been an accident." The Westwind was under a Martin Aviation certificate, so that is who operated the aircraft. I called up Bill Franke, who was on duty at that time and said, "Can you tell me what's going on?"

And, Bill says, "Yes, there has been an accident."

I was up in the bedroom with my wife when I turned on the news channel as I was talking to him on the phone. There was an on-scene camera showing wreckage from the accident. I immediately identified the tail number. "Bill," I said, "the airplane has crashed. I'm looking at the news. I can see the tail number."

The accident still plagues me today. On a professional and personal level, it was devastating.

At that time, there was not enough information about wake turbulence. So, the accident was just like a can falling off that pretend catering truck. There was nothing anybody could do about it. Nothing. The air traffic controller must have been devastated, but he couldn't predict what happened. He didn't know. He was just doing his job. But it was a very sad, sad event.

Back then, the knowledge of what aircraft was flying in front of you was not available. When you first called up the tower on the radio, you were only required to give your flight number or tail number, but you never identified what type of airplane you were flying.

They had never done testing on wake turbulence. And so, my thought, my hope, was that the way to alleviate accidents is to gain more knowledge and build a safety margin. I did that.

Giving the flight number of the plane just wasn't enough.

In airplane knowledge, a pilot used to call up the tower and say, "This is November 5652." And November 5652 might be a private 737, but if you're following that plane in a smaller aircraft then, that's like setting up United 757 and the Westwind all over again.

I came up with some observations and ideas. First, I thought the pilot should communicate the flight number and a Wake Turbulence Category: Heavy, Medium, and Light dependent on the Aircraft Prepared for Service weight (APS).

I contacted the FAA, the Flight Safety Foundation and spoke to anyone who would listen. I had meetings to get this idea out there, so they would change their philosophy.

After studying wake turbulence, I understood that the distance between aircraft should be increased. United 757 and the Westwind were just too close to each other. Distance between landing aircraft has been analyzed and increased since the accident from three to five miles.

My recommendation was adopted, and today, a pilot must label the type of aircraft he is flying. As a pilot, that information makes it much easier to get a clear picture of the sky around you: Okay, that's that large airplane there. There's a small airplane over there.

In the cockpit of an aircraft today, you also get proximity warnings. You can actually see where other airplanes are, based on your location. That was a significant change for the better. They tell you the type of aircraft, so you can better understand the landscape. That's a lot of difference.

But I would still like to see more stringent regulations about pilot training. It's getting there, but it's not entirely where I would like it to be. The more hours you have in an airplane is just like driving a car. When teenagers first get behind the wheel and pass their driver's license test, they tend to be cautious. Then, three or four months down the line, they start to feel more confident. That's when the accident happens, simply because they get overly confident and are still not as familiar or seasoned as they should be. That's when accidents happen.

The situation is the same with pilots and airplanes. The more time flying the aircraft, the better.

The accident changed the safety standards of the system for the better. The FAA allowed extra spacing between airplanes on landing, and pilots are alerted about the type and weight of airplanes in front of them. They never did that before. It was just flight numbers and who you were. You didn't know if it was a 747, 777, or a little airplane out for a cruise. You had no idea what the type of aircraft was. There are probably accidents that have been prevented and lives saved because of the changes in regulations that came from the In-N-Out Burger tragedy.

Because of that experience and our response, I started to build our own flight safety manual called the Air Carriers Commercial Operating Manual (ACCOM). We used to share that with our vendors. And that was when I met Lee Crowley from Nike, and I've worked on flight safety ever since. This accident shouldn't have happened. The two pilots flying these planes were experienced, but out of the sheer fluke . . .

The In-N-Out Burger crash was both personal and completely blindsiding. But I tried to take something extremely negative and very painful and find the detail, a lesson perhaps, that would help other people. That's how I operate. In the end, the accident had very far-reaching benefits for flight safety in both commercial and private air travel.

CHAPTER 13

Once-in-a-Lifetime

"Airspeed, altitude, and brains. Two are always needed to successfully complete the flight."

— Max Stanley, Northrop test pilot

I CAN REMEMBER TWO other events where I sat slack-jawed and brain-humming with next step possibilities. They were once-in-a-lifetime moments: September 11, 2001, and the rescue airlift after Hurricanes Katrina and Rita in 2005.

Both were tragedies.

The hurricanes were devastating natural disasters but primarily focused in the southern United States (Louisiana, Texas, and Mississippi). 9/11 was a human disaster and a terrorist act.

That was the major difference.

But the two ended up being similar because of the resources that were required after the event. The terrorist attack of 9/11 was more of a security crisis involving the entire country. I remember the day after 9/11. I happened to be in the city for a meeting, and I looked outside. There was nobody there. It was like Christmas Day, but in September. The streets were deserted, and I felt as if I was in the Twilight Zone.

The shock of what happened reverberated through the country, and everyone was looking for leadership and direction. The country's reaction after 9/11 was more akin to Pearl Harbor. Freedom. America lost some of its freedom that day.

I remember the morning starting off very typical, getting up early, getting dressed, preparing for my day. Then I turned the television on and immediately saw an angled shot of the World Trade Center. I was drawn to the screen when I saw that one of the towers was on fire.

This was not just another Tuesday. The exact details were not apparent yet, but my brain kicked into overdrive.

"That's rather a big fire; what's happened there?"

Then the reporter mentioned that a plane had flown into the building.

I was stumped. I'm an aviation fanatic, and I did not put two and two together that early in the morning. I observed and thought the situation through in purely practical terms.

"It's a clear day. How in the hell did a plane fly into that building?'"

The whole scene seemed ridiculous and made no sense to me. But the rolling news coverage possessed a building tension akin to a constantly evolving plot of a movie.

My attention was completely absorbed. Anyone who watched the events that day knows exactly how I felt. As you saw the action unfolding, you knew this was big. You just didn't exactly know why.

Mesmerized, I sat half-dressed at the edge of the bed, when suddenly, a second airplane — a Boeing 767, an aircraft that I knew inside out — slammed into the second tower of the World Trade Center.

This was no accident.

This I viscerally knew, and I went into full-blown emergency business mode. We had a couple of flights going out of New York that day, so I first called our communications center to find out what information we had. At that moment, the news was spotty at best. Everyone was grappling with the details, but I knew that we had to hold the two planned flights until we gained additional information and some clarity.

Within thirty-five or so minutes, we understood that a major terrorist attack was underway. The suggestion was floating that federal aviation authorities intended to shut down the entire United

States airspace to all traffic but military. Every plane was instructed to land at the closest available airport facility.

Now, whenever you start telling clients that their scheduled flight is delayed or canceled for whatever reason, it's never well-received, and there is usually a fair amount of blowback. "If you can't get me to my (fill in the blank) as scheduled, then why am I paying you?" But not that day. The news spread like wildfire. Something was seriously wrong and on a national scale. Every client we serviced that day, whether at airports or traveling to them, simply acknowledged our call, sat tight, or turned around and went home.

When I eventually got to the office, the scene was as tense as it was unique. The unfolding drama was morbidly captivating. Every employee stayed glued to the news channels while at the same time making every effort to get their day-to-day job done.

As the morning progressed, it became clear that the entire grid of United States airspace was going to grind to a halt for the first time in aviation history. Everything was being grounded. Every plane en route to the US from overseas was turned back, diverted to Canada, or to the closest airport that could accommodate them. This situation was unprecedented.

Predictably, we began to field calls from stranded clients still hoping to get to their destination. I hate to admit that we were somewhat stuck ourselves, and we just weren't in any position to respond to many of them.

One call came in from a gentleman who seemed to be under a great deal of pressure. He was perfectly lucid in what he was saying, but there was no mistaking the dire urgency in his voice. This was immediate, and possibly life or death. You could just hear it in his voice.

His corporate office had been in the second tower.

While he survived, he lost everything, including several members of his staff. In the center of this horrific scenario, he desperately needed to get back. I informed him that this was going to be a significant problem considering the closed airspace. I advised him to start driving, a rather bold and desperate suggestion I made for two specific reasons. First, we had no idea how long it would be until aircraft were up and running again. Second, at least he would be moving closer to his final destination as I made the necessary calls to see if we could do anything to help him.

I contacted one of our vendors in the Portland area and explained the situation. They informed me that they might be able to use an airplane located at an airbase in the Portland area, pending approval from the FAA.

That was a big pending *if*!

We initiated communications with the FAA, desperately trying to plead this gentleman's case. After numerous punts, I eventually was put in contact with a military command center. After speaking with one of their senior officers, explaining the full details of the story, and pleading this guy's predicament — especially that he had lost employees in the attack, the officer said he'd see what he could do and call me back as soon as possible.

I never thought I'd hear from him again.

In the meantime, I kept trying to get all possible updated information from the client by calling back and forth with the client as he drove the southbound freeway out of Seattle. At that point, we grasped that his drive path was taking him closer and closer to the airport where the plane we were trying to use was based.

Kudos to the military contact officer.

We actually did get a call back from the command center offering us something we hoped for but didn't realistically believe would be possible considering the situation.

We were granted a one-shot approval to fly this client out. And that's precisely what we did.

The day after, with the client having arrived safely in New York, I spoke to the crew who flew the plane. They told me how strange and surreal the flight had been. Usually, when a plane flies across the country, the crew contact and talk with people left, right and center, but on this September day, they spoke to no one at all. The reason?

Based on all our known information, this was the only non-military plane in the air. No contrails in the sky. Nothing. Just a single blip on the radar.

As the afternoon of September 11 dragged on, it became apparent that the commercial airline system wouldn't restart for several days. Planes were in the wrong places. Crews were in the wrong places. Everything was disorientated, upside down and backward.

We went from a situation where our phones in the office were totally quiet to suddenly being lit up all at once. People wanted to get back home or needed to get to their outbound destination for meetings, family, business. Everyone was calling us because executive aircraft was the fastest, most efficient option at that moment.

People were shaken. The security shortcomings of commercial aircraft had been so chillingly highlighted that passengers were willing to pay for the peace of mind that came with increased security. But, on the other hand, commercial airlines couldn't fly until all cockpit doors had been strengthened and secured. That's a lot of planes. Imagine how long that took.

After a week and a half, air travel was beginning to see some normalcy, but aircraft security has never been viewed the same again from that day to this. It's not that it wasn't taken seriously up until 9/11, but it just wasn't uniform: Private companies handled security, and security standards at one airport were often wildly different from others. The main priority was to make sure that every seat was filled. Other countries had already introduced security measures due to prior unfortunate circumstances: Israel, the United Kingdom. The UK was ahead of the curve because of terrorist issues and attacks associated with past experiences.

But for the United States, this was a new day. A different perspective. A loss of innocence.

An ironic afterword: the client we flew across the country that day bounced the payment on the flight. It was eventually settled up, but even if he hadn't, business took a back seat that day. In a catastrophe, help someone out. On September 11, 2001, all bets were off.

CHAPTER 14

The Call for Help

"Both optimists and pessimists contribute to our society. The optimist invents the airplane and the pessimist the parachute."

— Gil Stern

WHEN THE WATER IN the Gulf of Mexico feels just like the temperature of a warm bath, it may be fun to go in swimming, but, in the back of your mind, you can't help but think, "Oh perfect hurricane weather." Yeah. Absolutely. Weather is everything.

There's so much information that sparks through my brain when I talk about weather. We've done humanitarian evacuations for tornadoes. We've helped in hurricanes and typhoons, coordinated flights after tsunamis. Snowstorms. All weather-related. We have learned to hug the weather, because we're always running away or around or to meet it.

Commercial airlines shut down due to weather events not because they cannot operate the flight, but because it causes so much disruption. Consider a whole airline's system anywhere on the globe. If you are dealing with a weather phenomenon, let's say, going through Atlanta Hartsfield, then that messes everything up. If you put those airplanes elsewhere, then you're messing up your schedule. You don't have them ready for the next scheduled service. The crews aren't in the right place. It might take days to get the schedule all sorted out and back together again. So, the airline concludes that it is better to cancel the flight, leave the airplane there so you can engage immediately as soon as the weather lifts, then continue where you left off.

In the world of charter service, the weather is really not a problem for us as such. What's different about our system is that we can pierce around the weather. The weather is just like an obstacle. If it's snowstorms, then yes, we can get around snowstorms.

Does it make us money? Yes, it makes us huge amounts of money. Do we deliver on our promise of getting the client to their destination? Is it great for our customers? Absolutely, because we can work around the weather. We can see the storms.

We are in communication with the airport. Is it open? If not, where can we go to? If not there, perhaps we can go to another airport maybe forty miles away. Weather is hugely influential to our business and to what we do. We are more flexible and adaptable than any commercial airline will ever be.

If there is some type of disaster, and we can't get into our planned airport, then we can work around and get in as close as possible. As the airport in the affected area opens up, then we can start to fly in.

The first thing on the agenda is always to open the airport.

Does that cause problems? Yes, but we always find a solution. Just because a weather event is happening here doesn't mean it is affecting over there.

It's like the forest fires that we work on. We support the firefighters on the front line. We've worked getting personnel in early and bringing them out in the nick of time. We have to quickly change plans if we can't get them to, or out of, a prearranged spot. Where can we get these firefighters in to put the fires out? Then we'll get them in, and they move.

We've done a lot of emergency fire relief over the years. When there is a fire, you first have to move firefighters into remote locations to put out the fire, but often you can't get into that area. Or you've got to move equipment into place, but you can't get in because the land belongs to the military. Or it's closed. Or something else is going on.

Where is the next place you can move them? And then, you need ground transportation to get them to the final destination. Does that work? We can get you nearby. That works fine. Get us in there. So that's where you're talking and listening to the client.

Here in California, basically they have a hold or base, like a MASH camp. When the fires are raging, there's this whole flurry of activity, fire engines, people, structures, and command centers. They just go in and set everything up. Two weeks after the fire is out, the whole area looks like a campground again. You would never know anything happened. During the fire, it looks like mission control.

One of the strengths of Le Bas is our ability to deal with a changing environment, tap into the flexibility of charter aircraft, and the talent to forecast the next change.

We've assisted with many natural disasters over the years. You name it, we've done it.

We helped during the California earthquake, the San Francisco one, and that was the year before we even started Le Bas International. We were flying people left, right, center, and up and down from Los Angeles up to San Francisco and back.

When the tsunami occurred the day after Christmas in 2004, so horribly affecting beach communities in Indonesia, Thailand, and Sri Lanka, we were involved in moving heavy equipment over there to help clear the debris. We moved helicopters over to help the search and rescue teams that didn't have enough lift.

We've worked with the FAA and DOT, the TSA, and even foreign governments. That's what we do every day. That's part of our job to the point that we have a separate program called humanitarian lift, that is specially dedicated to disaster relief.

When a request comes through to Le Bas, we have a team that is specifically trained to move the request forward. A dedicated team does that. We've moved personnel, emergency supplies, and specialized emergency canine units to all kinds of locations, so we are familiar with bidding on these jobs, and more importantly, getting the work done.

Enter Hurricanes Katrina and Rita.

When I first saw the beginnings of what eventually became Hurricane Katrina, I seriously thought that there might be a potential for something catastrophic. We had already facilitated with hurricane/typhoon relief in the past, and I've always had a keen interest in tracking hurricanes. With my aviation eye on weather patterns, I would study the charts and data to make my own predictions on the path of a particular storm and where it was most likely to make landfall.

I remember that I first noticed the disturbance that became Hurricane Katrina via Intellicast.com, a fantastic global web based underground weather channel.

Using this service, I can track storms starting way out in the Pacific or down by Mexico, but especially off the coast of Africa, because that's where the storms most likely to hit the United States form. They generate there, start spinning up, and trail gradually towards the Caribbean. Depending on the water temperature, they either head north or go into the Gulf of Mexico.

During hurricane season but especially during the months of August and September, I always keep a lookout for the storms coming inbound. I would often instruct our team to put a hold on planes near what might be an affected area because of probable evacuations. I also based it on possible requirements and who we might be working with.

The U.S. Federal Emergency Management Agency (FEMA) is a special section of the Department of Homeland Security and is responsible for the emergency response to natural disasters. It has learned a lot from the scenario that developed from Hurricanes Katrina and Rita, which were both terribly unusual. The two storms were right behind each other and that was uncommon. They even followed the same track, which is even more rare. But the phenomena were attributed to water temperature.

Basically, I could see this disturbance chugging up by Wednesday or Thursday, the week before, so I put in a call to LandStar, an international transportation and logistics company whose corporate headquarters are in Jacksonville, FL. They had a contract with FEMA. I also contacted several other organizations we reached out to during disaster relief, and I asked one simple question, "Do you guys see this thing coming in?"

They said, "Yes." and I said, "Do you possibly think that any rescue airplanes might be needed?" I received a negative reply and let it go.

Thursday came along and this storm was still building, going down below Cuba, and intensifying all the way. I made phone calls every morning, "Hey guys, have you seen this thing barreling through?" I reached out to multiple contacts, both private companies and government entities, to try to get a handle on what behind-the-scenes planning was going on.

One of the associates I reached out to was Mike Whitman, a very good friend of mine, who then managed his own weather service company. He's an unbelievable weatherman, a complete guru who has an expert read on the atmospheric situation. If he was on the television, you'd know exactly what the weather was going to be.

I'll segue to two brief stories about Mike Whitman...

Over the years, we've been involved in a few conferences for the Ford Motor Company. One such conference involved transporting approximately 350 radio station DJs from all over California to unique locations to drive the new line of Ford cars.

And so, we'd go to these unusual remote airports in the middle of nowhere.

Local airport operators had to take a sharp breath during this event because airplanes would be landing and taking off every five minutes, where generally at these airports, there might be an airplane taking off once a day.

The very first time we handled transportation for the event, it was into the middle of the desert, and it had been raining in California for about forty-one days. Rain every single day. The coordinators were building a facility that resembled a movie set, and all the people invited to the conference expected to test drive the cars.

Everybody was getting really, really, super nervous.
I called up Mike and said, "Mike. Take a look." You know, I called him beforehand because I was getting nervous myself. I mean, we had spent months and months putting this together. After examining the weather patterns, he said, "Nope. In the early hours of the morning, you'll see clear. It'll be sunshine." I drove down there myself. God bless him. Pools of water everywhere and then there it was. Stars.

The second occasion we did the conference was up in Mammoth. Same thing with possible inclement weather. Snowstorms were coming in, blizzards. There I was, sitting in the ski lodge with all the Ford people, and watching the brand-new cars parked right outside get pelted with snow buffeting in at right angles.

They all turned and looked at me and I said, "It's going to be okay."

Once again, I had spoken to Mike. Once again, I set my alarm to get up and check at two o'clock in the morning. Truth be told, I didn't have to set my alarm, I was already awake. I pulled the curtain back and looked out the window. Nothing. No additional snow. The conference planners had to get extra people in to clear the snow off the cars, but the event went off without a hitch.

The weather was picture perfect. Again, just like a movie set. The attendees arrived to a picturesque scene in snow covered mountains where they were going to have the time of their lives driving cars off-road in fresh snow. What more could you want? Did I do this? Well, maybe I did. I don't know!

Back to natural disasters and Hurricane Katrina and Rita . . .

I called Mike because I am always curious about the weather. I didn't really understand how these storms form, but I did know that it was water related. I talked it out with him. He concurred, "Yes, you're dead right. That is how it generates."

A hurricane acts like a vacuum. On one end, the vacuum sucks everything up, and the other end begins to swirl, displacing everything, and spitting it out again. Tornados, wave surge and the subsequent flooding cause most of the destruction. Most of the devastation is attributed to water rather than wind.

I asked him, "Where do you see this thing going?" He examined the possibilities and yes, confirmed that it would be a major hurricane that would have severe consequences on the Mississippi Gulf Coast and New Orleans metro area.

I called up my contacts yet again and said, "Guys, anything happening?"

And their response was still a pointed, "No." This was on Friday. Then on Saturday the same: "Anybody have anything?"

"No."

Sunday was the same thing.

All the while, I watched this behemoth turn and take aim on the Mississippi Gulf Coast and New Orleans metro area.

I could not ignore the obvious any longer. We put airplanes on standby, all that our company could. All without being requested. On our own. We knew it was going to be big.

And the reason why nothing was activated was because the two governors of Louisiana and Mississippi were sitting on their hands. FEMA can only get involved when you declare an emergency. I think it was a bit harsh for everybody to blame FEMA. Those two governors didn't declare a national emergency, so FEMA could not get involved.

Otherwise, FEMA would have been more ready. Emergency relief could have been put in place well in advance. That was the real reason why it didn't get there in time.

Hurricane Katrina made landfall on August 29, 2005. Sunday night, and then Monday morning and continuing throughout the entire day on Monday. Believe it or not, a state of emergency was still not declared.

I was just about ready to leave the office and go home late on Monday afternoon when I got a call. One of our contacts said, "We need eight airplanes for tomorrow. We need to evacuate seven and a half thousand people." And I said, "Holy shit, and you call at this time of day?"

The pressing need for evacuation and support started to build gradually from there. We put the call out for aircraft until we ran out of airplanes. I mean, you just can't pull airplanes big enough to carry that many people that quickly along with crews and everything else.

There was one carrier, and I'll be diplomatic in not naming them, a big American carrier, a huge one who didn't offer any assistance whatsoever. I made the phone call and the lady on duty said to me, "No, we have nothing."

I implored, "Do you realize what it's for?"

She repeated, "Nope. We can't help you. We've nothing."

We pulled airplanes from every single large carrier we do business with in the United States to assist. By Tuesday, we also started to receive private requests for charter evacuation.

The very first charter we did in the New Orleans area was for a doctor. We flew into the smaller Lakefront airport and the family had to get through the city to the airport by boat. As we landed, the family walked across the ramp, got on the airplane, and we left. We got a lovely letter from them thanking us. I still have it.

When we got to the small airport, we soon realized that there was a complete disconnect between what we were hearing on the news or from officials and what the reality of the situation was. The place was destroyed, all the normal everyday services just weren't there. All the people had left. There was no one at that airport.

The first thing that was needed was for the government to get the military in there to help reopen and run the airport. We originally had all these flights scheduled, but the main airport, the big one — Louis Armstrong International — was not operational.

In addition, we also realized we didn't have support and TSA people there. The very first mission was to bring TSA people in from other places to assist with the passengers.

Then we had to wait for necessary infrastructure to be put in place. There were no stairs to board the aircraft, nothing, and no one on the ground to help us out. We had to get all that in place before we could do anything to help out. I still offer big congratulations and kudos to everyone who was involved in that operation because it was a monumental task to get that airport operational.

But then, in the background, there was another storm brewing. Hurricane Rita was heading towards Texas.

We were dealing with lots of things: infrastructure, personnel, another storm, and people grappling with all of that to make things happen.

A critical piece of information that we didn't fully appreciate until a call later that week was that everything had to be flown in - the crews, airplanes, and everything we were working with. There was nothing there. Nowhere to stay. Nothing to eat. We had to come in and take people out after the workday was done, rotating to assist evacuees from New Orleans who were going all over the United States!

Another issue that presented later that week was a problem with the departing schedule.

We were supposed to have all the airplanes there relatively early, but the flights were leaving late after midday, way off schedule. We had been sitting there ready to go since eight o'clock in the morning and we had no idea why there were delays. Near the end of the week, we suddenly were able to work out the issue: the buses were not able to load and couldn't leave because of the strict curfew in the city.

The buses couldn't board and go to the airport until the curfew was lifted.

After we found out about that, we said, "Guys, move it up." And after they did, we managed to get a lot more people out of there.

Again, hats off to everybody who did what was needed to support the mission. It was truly an incredible undertaking.

On a human level, many of the airport employees had lost their homes and their own families were in trouble. There was no gas, no nothing, no services, no lights and still they performed their job admirably.

A difficulty that manifested after day two, really after day one, was that we ran out of airplanes. So, we spoke with the Department of Transportation on the phone, which is very rare. Normally in each country, you are not allowed to bring in aircraft from foreign countries because it's in your domicile. But since we had run out of planes, we asked the DOT, "Can we reach out to our brotherhood in Canada?" Surprisingly, they said. "Absolutely."

We started speaking to the Canadians who pretty much scoffed and said, "This is never going to happen. You know, we can't operate down there."

We kept at it and asked, "What do you need to get it done? What do you need if you have aircraft and you can break an airplane loose or break two airplanes loose to help us out, what do you need to get them done?"

And they responded, "We need a letter from the DOT."

For each airline that had availability, we got the DOT to write out the letter of permission they required. The Canadians were astounded. They said, "We never heard of this." Bringing Canadian operators all the way down to New Orleans to evacuate people had never been done before. Never, not at all.

Starting on Tuesday of that week, we used any aircraft we could grab. The evacuation continued through the week, lasting for six or seven days.

By that time, disaster officials were able to bring in buses. They established fuel points in areas where there were no gas stations and they were able to put in fuel valves, so the buses were able to operate.

On that Thursday, in the midst of a multitude of airplanes coming in and heading back out again, President George W. Bush decided to make a presidential tour of the disaster area. We were already flying that morning when we got the alert that the president was inbound. Again, a lack of communication.

When there's a presidential airplane coming inbound, all other aircraft are kept far away for security reasons. It meant that we couldn't land at the airport. All our incoming airplanes were kept in a holding pattern.

No fault . . . The president wanted to, even needed to see the disaster area.

But the planners probably should have flown him to a place farther out so he wouldn't jam up the air space. The poor guys working at the air base down there in New Orleans were stressed enough. They were using emergency ancillary communications, when suddenly, they got the word that Air Force One was coming down. Imagine this whole balloon of an area where you can't fly, and you can't land.

We literally had airplanes running out of fuel, pushing hours of crew duty, and it was not like everyone wasn't frazzled to the hilt already. The pilots were calling us, saying "What do you want us to do? We have to go somewhere to land. Which flight are we going to delay? Are we going to delay all of them? Can we have any service at all today?"

Here I must salute Donough Hughes who is now the Chief Operating Officer (COO) of Le Bas International. He was the key person who pulled the scheduling chaos together that day. I've known Donough for a very long time. He and his wife are tremendous people, and he won a well-deserved award for his work. This was such a massive operation.

In the world of past disaster, no two relief events are ordinary following hurricanes Katrina and Rita. Le Bas International choreographed the largest civilian airlift since World War II. Seven thousand was only the beginning. Literally a drop in an ocean.

During the humanitarian mission, Le Bas transformed problems of scarce supply, limited resources, bureaucratic regulations, and basic security into a rescue opportunity.

Nobody knew how many people needed help. No one knew what to expect. The scene was like a canvas. You only recognized what the artwork might be when you started to paint. These first responders and our own personnel were only able to decide what needed to be done when they got further into the undertaking.

Authorities were going through each neighborhood to mark the houses derelict or clear, to rescue those who needed aid, or recover the dead. They were combing through the various wards of the city followed by buses needed to evacuate stranded survivors.

FEMA wasn't working to a plan. They had no plan. And that was not to say that was bad, but the situation was so completely unprecedented. They had never before had to deal with the enormity of the disaster, or the sheer number of people in dire need.

FEMA coordinated the destinations of the evacuation flights. Texas was a major stop point until under the Texas government halted the flow of evacuees under the threat of Hurricane Rita. Not only were they running out of shelters and places to put people, but they were also forced to move their own citizens inland.

So, we began flying people farther west and north, to get them out of the way of the oncoming storm in Texas. FEMA did a tremendous job speaking to governmental entities in each state to coordinate the evacuees.

FEMA organized what essentially became a national outreach. California didn't think they'd be involved. Neither did Montana, or many other states. They didn't dream they'd have people coming in from Louisiana or Texas during emergency disaster relief. But this wasn't just a natural disaster, it was a natural human disaster.

Near the end of our evacuation effort for Hurricane Katrina, there were the strangest people getting on airplanes. Some turned up with their pet snakes. The crew was like, "Hang on a second here."

Can you imagine?

"Excuse me, the lady in 23D, could you just put your snake away? You're making the other passengers tense."

Quite a few passengers would not board without their animals. At that point, we just shrugged. Okay, this is New Orleans, we get it.

Rita followed so close on the heels of Katrina that both hurricanes still seemed like one continual rolling catastrophe, like one of those Christmas parcels that you open up to find another box inside then another box inside of that. All hands-on deck were working at their maximum output.

I stayed in the office. We sent out for pizza and tea and coffee — whatever the staff needed. We stole naps when we could, maybe went home for a shower a couple of times, then immediately came back. We were locked in the office start to finish for about eleven days.

At the same time, we were also working on our executive side. Corporations stopped running in anticipation of the coming storm. They didn't have their records, documents. As soon as they understood they were in harm's way, they started calling. We had a lot of people moving out of there on executive airplanes as well. Every single person in the disaster zone was affected.

These two storms were unprecedented. Once a national emergency was declared, the evacuation channels were already backed up. The boat had already left. We were just working the recovery.

Each weather event is unique. The terrain is unique. Floods are unique. Hurricanes, typhoons are all unique. But I would suggest that as these events have become more commonplace, the services needed in response are becoming more precise and tactful.

For example, FEMA had houses built and sent down, only to have nobody use them. The houses sat for months and months, then years. Nobody used them, and the reason they stayed empty was because FEMA didn't realize that there was no electricity and nowhere to plug them in. There were no roads to get to them, no infrastructure to service them. The place was completely devastated.

But they did learn from that experience. When a natural disaster is that big, it does no good moving goods to the survivors. The people must be evacuated so the neighborhoods can be restructured and rebuilt from the inside out.

I think there needs to be more self-accountability in the evacuation process and better communication about the impending disaster all around. In Europe, alarm warnings are given according to the severity, starting from a yellow alert on up.

Consider an aviation windsock. A pilot knows how to estimate the wind according to what the windsock is doing.

In the United States, there is a tremendous amount of discretion about the timing of the official "Evacuate" order. They leave it too much to the general public and the news channels feed you bits of information from their station because that means more advertising, more money. And the government entities are cautious about calling for an evacuation because that means business closures and loss of revenue as well. There needs to be more cooperation from the government and more responsibility from the media.

In the end, how many lives did we save? How many lives were saved because of FEMA? How many because of the Red Cross? Because of the pilots? Or the TSA? Or because of the volunteers that came in to help from all around the world?

I don't believe in the masses. I always say that if you lose sight of a penny, you lose sight of a dollar. It's the same with people. Every individual person brings something to the planet. Our passengers went through a traumatic experience. They wanted to get out. They needed to get out. That was what we did, and it was very humbling to be of service to them.

CHAPTER 15

Personal Touch to the Test

"The only mystery in life is why the kamikaze pilots wore helmets." — Al McGuire

I HAVE A SAYING that I use quite often: "If you can't provide excellent customer service, don't provide it at all." Personal touch in our customer service is a cornerstone at Le Bas. Still, there are circumstances that put even me to the test.

There was that other hurricane, Hurricane Hortense, a Category 4 storm with 137 mph winds that made landfall on September 3, 1996, in Guadeloupe and Puerto Rico. The damage was devastating at $158 million.

Hurricane Hortense interfered with a carefully planned and well-rehearsed event for one of our satellite clients who owns a very big space company.

We assisted in launch protocol festivities by arranging for companies and guests to travel to South America to view rocket launch liftoffs. I was responsible for this one particular flight.

We took off and went down on the first flight of the journey. Everything was perfect. I mean, this sheepdog had done his job. Not only had he put all the sheep in the pen, but he put a ribbon around each one of the sheep, a pink ribbon.

An official countdown to a rocket launch takes twenty-one days. That was what it took back then for one of these rockets to prepare for liftoff. So, twenty-one days out, we finalized detailed plans about what would happen. Everything was sealed in place. I flew down to Miami meeting Dr. Richard Pitts, my wife's good friend and her boss at the time. We met the night prior at the hotel restaurant. At the same time of the arriving aircraft. Miami had just gone through a hurricane watch, and when I looked at the weather, another storm was boring up the Caribbean.

I got a call at 2:00 a.m. saying that the airplane we had booked couldn't do the charter. Apparently, the overnight trajectory of the hurricane path passed over the flight plan routing, wiping out the entire ground navigation systems. These systems must be operational to fly down there.

The only way to circumvent the problem was to go south, around the islands, all the way around. We just didn't have the time for that. Again, everything was set. The people were there and waiting. The rocket was on countdown.

We scrambled. I remember being on the phone in the lobby. This was for a cutting-edge satellite company, and we had eighty VIP passengers. The CEO's wife took a photograph of me on the phone, trying to sort this out with the operations center.

Eventually, we did manage to get an airplane, but it was nothing like the airplane we had originally commissioned, which had six staterooms up in the front of the fuselage with a bar strategically placed in the middle. It would have been a first-class transport similar to an old private railcar from an earlier era. The aircraft was a work of art, just beautiful.

The aircraft we did take on short notice was all economy. If the other plane was a state car, this one was a boxcar. In fact, the replacement airplane had three different color schemes on the outside. The interior was filled with different seats all the way through. It looked like something out of Monty Python.

I was hyperventilating. "Oh, my goodness gracious."

That was the beginning, and it didn't stop. It just didn't stop.

Next, we dealt with a six-hour delay on a VIP flight. Then, finally, we committed to using this aircraft after checking everything out.

We took off, intending to use the same catering, but the food had spoiled. There was nothing I could do about it. No amount of sheep-dogging can conjure eighty first-class meals during a flight. You just can't do it. It is not possible.

The plane's crew reminded me of my days in Zambia Airways because it was a United Nations crew. They were terrific, doing the best they could with what they had available. On the way down to French Guiana, we received word of another issue.

Workers in that part of the world do pick the most opportune time to go on strike.

Often when a rocket launch is scheduled in this part of the world, that's when local workers decide to go on strike because guests are coming into town. That's a time when they receive the most publicity and can best make their demands known.

For example, the bus transportation people were on strike, and they blocked the roads to the airport with buses which was a massive inconvenience. You could only get in and out by helicopter or by somehow getting around the blocked roads while the airport was closed.

As we were flying down, I looked out of the window, and all I could see was this monster storm as far out to the horizon as possible. When you're flying at 32,000 feet, looking out the window, and seeing this hurricane, all you can say is, "Holy crap." It was a monster, and I was so wound up, I felt the adrenaline pumping.

Before we began our landing approach, I received a message to come to the cockpit. So, I made my way to the front, went into the cockpit, and put the headphones on. And the airport authority was calling over the HF in a rather frantic voice. "You can't come over there. *Monsieur,* you cannot come to French Guiana. The airport is closed."

This was not what I wanted to hear. I'm like, "What? What do you mean?" And I'm pretty sure I also said, "Crap, what do we do?"

Luckily, we had camaraderie in the cockpit. The pilot was absolutely fantastic. He was German, an ex-Eastern Airlines captain. When he turned up at the airport in Miami, I wanted to give him a hug because there he was, very Eastern Airlines, immaculately dressed and ready to fly. "Oh my God, am I pleased to see you." I nearly cried.

He calmed me down, and we talked about it. We started a repertoire and decided to divert from the course to fly to Saint Lucia. We landed safely, and then I had another immediate challenge.

Where do I find eighty hotel rooms?

I think when something goes wrong, it is more challenging to get your point of view across to the opposite side, saying that this is what I feel. But I think the real gift is to negotiate and listen together to find a positive, workable solution.

In other words, nobody likes it when things go wrong, right? You're not here for things to get messed up. So, it might be a technical problem, or something happens with the schedule or the weather. Nobody likes that, so what can you do positively? I think that's an art to say, "Well, breaks, breaks, breaks, breaks. What's on the table in front of us, and what can we do to make sense of it?" If you don't have anything new at the table, that's fine. Give us a moment to think it out, and then talk it through with the client.

Manage we did.

We booked eighty hotel rooms. And we went off that night. The airport in French Guiana opened in the morning, and we were able to fly in. But, again, it took a lot of sheepdogging to get in there.

At this point in the journey, most of the clients understood that circumstances were beyond our control, but they still were somewhat frustrated.

Luckily, the special guests did arrive safely and on time. Imagine a James Bond movie with a slice of Hawaii, then add the French road systems and a heaping dose of Louisiana. Finally, blend that all together in a big mixing bowl. That's what French Guiana is like.

As you fly into French Guiana, you go overland, make a right-hand turn to come into land at the airport, and you see the mists of South America. There's nothing like it. Not in Africa or anywhere else. It is both unique and very precious.

After you've seen the Amazon, you look at the earth in a whole different light. You can literally, just beyond one of the roads that connect the city to the launchpad, stop and walk two meters into the jungle, and you can't see anything. It's all green.

The rocket launch site and the support facility are a massive, state-of-the-art infrastructure in the middle of the jungle. The auditorium for guests and scientists has seats all the way around like a theatre. A glass "real-time" viewing area of the launch site and colossal television screens showing all the people working on the countdown in mission control. So, there is a countdown: five, four, three, two, one, and all the stats of the rocket are displayed. And then for a moment, there's nothing . . .

Watching an Ariane 5 or an Ariane 4 going up, every single hair on your body vibrates, and you respond. You involuntarily stand up. The sound is like the space shuttle, with a distinctive crackle as if the air itself is alive. There is so much energy there. It's unbelievable.

After this rocket went up, the company's CEO made his speech. And he was in tears, simply because of what just happened. He had his whole family, his baby, his wife, there with him. They had been on the airplane. And it may have been difficult, but we delivered. We still made it happen.

On the first day you arrive, you usually go to the hotel and get settled. Then, in the evening, the company hosts a party, a meet and greet where they can explain the launch. After that, the visitors go to the gantry and tour the facility the next day. And then they truck off to Devil's Island, the infamous prison made famous in the film *Papillon*. Why do people go and visit prisons? It's just like the one in the middle of San Francisco Bay, but that's what they do.

Then the next day is launch day.

Due to prevailing winds, rockets tend to go up in the evening because it's calm, and there's less weather, storms, or anything like that. Unfortunately, the timing of rocket launches is governed by the timing of hitting a precise orbital position in time and space, requiring them to hit a pre-calculated window for liftoff. If the weather is not right when that window arrives, then they just don't launch. That's why the rockets in Cape Canaveral go up at night or in the morning because of better atmospheric conditions.

If there's a launch delay due to a technical problem, they'll wait for 24 hours, and the guests will come back. If it doesn't go the next day, the guests still return. Rocketry is still an experimental science.

On the night of the rocket launch, the company's CEO was talking, and many of the guests thought it was pretty bad form when he said, "Thank you very much for being down here. I know it's been very hard. It wasn't what we desired." And then he said, "If our charter company can get us back to Miami safely . . ."

I was in the room, and people were looking at me. Some from Japan and other parts of the world. I kind of thought that his comment made me feel as if I wasn't doing what I was trying to do. I had everyone there safely and on time. They still got to see the launch.

On the way back, we again had to deal with the strikes. We also worked out how to get around the buses and get to the airport. But the problem was, nobody else could get to the airport. No catering. No fuel. We had nothing. The only place we could go to stop was en-route to pick up fuel but that meant we would be over landing weight getting there.

The crew and I had another pow-wow. How do we accomplish this? I mean, we were stuck. No pushback tug. But given a bit of time, we figured out a solution: we offloaded the restroom water to give us the correct landing weight. Sounds simple now.

Our pilot was an outstanding fellow. And there you are. Time and again, I've witnessed this, and it is not an unusual thing. This is something I've lived with all my life. You must develop the ability to think outside the box.

After we figured that out and got to the airport, we had to find a pair of steps, but we did. We'd got them up to the plane, and we got the door open. Luckily, the airplane had its internal power, so we powered up. Air traffic control was there because they couldn't get home, so they stayed there.

We've had so many problems down there over the years, but probably the last time I left, I said, "I'm sorry. I'm not coming back, even though it's a fantastic thing." There have been so many strikes down there over the years. In fact, we've even got bills from companies that provided no services because they went on strike, but they charged us anyway. They didn't perform the handling service. So, I'm like, "What's wrong with this picture?"

We picked up fuel and headed back to Miami. I was thinking, "Wouldn't it be nice if we were on the ground when I said we'd be on the ground." We had a bet going, so I went to the cockpit and spoke with the captain.

I said, "I want us to beright on time."

He said, "I'll tell you what, I'm going to slow the airplane down. You're going to be on stand exactly the second and the minute that you said we were going to be on stand."

I went back to my seat, but I could hardly sit still. I was nearly in tears because the amount of stress was phenomenal. With help from my traveling companion friend Dr. Pitt, we wrote a message. Then I went back into the cockpit, wondering when was the best time to deliver the message?

The best time was just as we pulled the power back; it's nice and quiet. I went on the microphone and said, "First of all, I wanted to say to our customers, congratulations on the momentous rocket launch. This hurricane has put us to the test, and sometimes, we pass the test. But our main thought was to get you there and back safely and to have you witness the launch. The storm was out of everybody's hands, but I want to thank you all for being with us."

And I didn't hear this because I was in the cockpit, but everybody in the airplane was applauding. And yes, we got on the stand. Right on that stand.

But human beings are funny enough. That reminds me of two other launch stories. People are so distractable, so unpredictable.

Once at Cape Canaveral, guests were touring this legendary rocket launch facility, and there was a golden eagle up in the nest at the top of a telegraph pole. Everyone was looking at the golden eagle, not at what they came to see.

The same happened in French Guiana with several rocket launches. The launch site was in the distance, all lit up at night, and the guests were in the viewing facility, about five miles from the rocket launch.

The rocket is gearing up, ready to go. All the guests have headphones, and based on their native language, all commentary translates into the language you can understand. You can hear the launch and the commands being given. The rocket takes off. Spectacular.

Maybe about forty-five seconds into the launch, somebody says, "Hey, look at this spider."

Of course, the spiders in the Amazon are impressive, but $165 million was taking off and going up in the sky, the most giant firework you'll ever see, and they wanted to look at a spider.

This palpable wave of energy from the launch hit us, vibrating like no tomorrow against our bodies, and everybody stared at the spider. Were the guests crazy? No, just human.

CHAPTER 16

Deliver the Monster

*"Every piece of cargo is precious to somebody somewhere.
They want and wait for it . . . Somewhere."*
— Tracey Deakin

Cargo is a monster nowadays, especially with Amazon, Federal Express, and other wholesale and retail online sellers that rely on quick, efficient service. On any given day, Le Bas delivers on cargo transport, but in a very different and specialized way.

If we can fit it in the airplane, we'll make it happen. You name it, we've moved it. I have had the honor of offering air cargo transport services for vital machinery, satellite components, hazmat equipment, precious art, and even gold bullion.

We've brought human organs to patients waiting for transplant surgery lots of times.

I remember one gentleman who contacted me when I was with Alpha Jet. He was quite the unusual fellow, about five foot nine, stocky, dark trousers, tee shirts, but wearing a jacket. Though a bit scruffy and slightly overweight, this man was responsible for transporting a lot of the human organ transplants from the originating hospital to the receiving hospital - emergency room to theatre. This was before organ transplant centers even existed. Later on, we did work for them as well.

This gentleman used to have five pagers on him, all from various hospitals, and they sounded like tubular bells every time they went off. We would all jump like, "What the hell is going on?" Via our own specialized Medevac Learjet, we transported a complete flight team, including a nurse and everything else that was necessary to bring patients safely home.

We did a lot of that, and we also moved other essential medical supplies. Even though it's not done anymore, we used to rush radioactive isotopes to treat cancer patients. The isotopes were injected into a patient's vein to allow the medical team to see the cancer. The isotopes had a very short half-life, so transporting the material was stat and needed to move quickly.

We've also done a lot of work for Shriners pediatric hospital in Texas that treats severely burned kids. The entire hospital is dedicated to pediatric care and especially burn victims. If a child suffers from severe burns — it doesn't matter where they are in the world - we've flown them to this hospital, and it's paid for. The hospital exists for the sole purpose of taking care of these kids.

Retracing all the way back to my days at Invicta, we used to load what was called bulk cargo. Everything was literally loaded by hand, piece by piece, just like you do in a garage. Here, here, and here. The aircraft didn't have mechanized floor systems as they have now.

So, when I began loading cargo, it was vital to learn how to distribute weight and understand where the cargo could be placed on the airplane. Everything had to be weighed before bringing it on the planes.

I was working for Invicta at Manston when I saw my first gold shipment. The flight, operated by Swiss Air using a McDonnell Douglas DC-9-10F, brought gold bullion from Switzerland to London. The door was open on the airplane, and as I went up the stairs, I saw nine pallets full of gold.

Our office would receive a phone call the day before the flight was expected. There was no security as such. There was no security because it just turned up, so there wasn't enough time to arrange for increased security. At the time, nobody thought much of anything about it. It was just a job. The gold came in on the airplane and was moved to waiting bullion trucks for a trip to the mint in England.

But I was like a kid in a candy store. I can still picture it now, like I can all the cargo we've flown. Everything from spaceship bits to animals, you name it. I can see it all. I remember standing at the cargo door near the cockpit and looking into the back of the plane. The entire cargo bay was filled with gold. Shiny stuff.

My work with cargo at Invicta was an essential building block of what I do today with our airline services program. When somebody tells me what they want to ship, I can visualize the dimensions in my brain, and I know what airplane we will use. I might be getting a bit foggier now because I don't do it day-in-and-day-out anymore but, I can still basically design the job.

If the cargo is over a certain weight, a larger pallet, like a spreader board, will be required to equalize the weight out over a bigger distance. If it's too long, I'll put it in the nose loader airplane or turn the cargo around in the plane. Maybe the size seems prohibitive, but when you get inside, you can rotate it around the door to get it all the way in the airplane.

I like it when a request is different or complex, or when someone throws me an unusual curveball because I don't give up. I'm like a dog with a bone. Like, "Grr. It's down there somewhere." I won't put it down. I'm like a pig finding truffles. My nose tells me it's down there somewhere. I'm going to get it. I will find a way to accomplish the task.

Often, because of my experience, I just know what to do. I don't have to think about it, and in that respect, I'm like a pilot. A good pilot has an instinct; he doesn't have to do the checklist. The checklist is there just to make sure he doesn't miss something. But he already knows what to check and what he's looking for.

So, I like those complicated, unusual requests because it challenges my brain to think.

We often move airplane engines for airlines. I remember one cargo flight that was bringing an engine halfway across the world, but there was a problem. The engine was on a Russian airplane, and it didn't have the authority or clearance to fly in the United States.

So, we came up with a solution.

We decided to use the Hercules, an American turboprop transport aircraft, to meet the Russian jet plane on an island somewhere in the Caribbean. We landed both on the ramp and then backed them up against each aircraft's tail section. We pulled the engine off one, slid it into the cargo hold of the other, and took off again.

That plan worked and it was all within the price that the client wanted.

These unusual tasks are what we're meant to do. We face situations like this every single day. That's the job of our people and why we're called upon to help.

Many high-priority items move by air charter, simply because the production line behind them cannot be stopped. So, if you're Ford or Toyota or whoever and you've got a piece of equipment essential to a production line, then air charter is the answer.

We've moved diamond and gold drill bits all the way to Papua New Guinea.

If a company needs a specialized tool like this for drilling, what happens if it gets busted? They've got all these people waiting on the payroll. They will not be drilling for anything until this piece gets repaired. They are in the same situation as a company with a production line, like Boeing, because profits will take a hit. If production and manufacturing grind to a complete standstill, that can easily cost millions of dollars a day.

But the same situation can exist for a pair of shoes.

One of the biggest conventions in Las Vegas is the annual shoe convention. It's ginormous, totally massive. I wasn't even aware of it until we got a call one day.

Would you believe that we were hired to move one pair of shoes from Honolulu to Las Vegas?

The shoes were meant to be shipped express overnight, high priority, and were somehow missed by mistake. But the dealer needed them for the show. Someone called us in a total panic and said, "Oh God, we need the shoes."

This happens every day. It's not wholly unusual. I had no idea the shoe business was that big, but if the shoes weren't there, then they couldn't sell them. This was not an option.

We had to get them to Las Vegas from Hawaii. Okay, so done.

To anyone reading this story, you're probably thinking, "Well, that's ridiculous! You move shoes in an executive airplane?! Are you joking?" But if you look at what the shoe business is, how massive it is, and then consider that this Las Vegas show only happens once a year, then yes. Add to that fact, all the buyers go there to forecast and buy products for the following year. This doubles the importance. If you've spent X amount of time, effort, materials, and brain thought creating these shoes, and they're not where they're meant to be? Suddenly it looks like a small price to pay.

That's the leading edge. That's the excitement of it all.

Every day, I look at our board and see what we've got coming in. Every single request is a low-hanging piece of fruit with a lovely bit of a challenge. It's like a pear coated in fresh morning dew, that is saying, "Eat me, eat me! But to pick me, you have to win the test first." You're thinking, "Oh, look, that's going to be so good and juicy." But you can't have it yet, not until you figure out how to pluck it from the branch.

We've done a lot of stuff for movies over the years. We often co-ordinate the scout trip that takes place before a movie crew goes out to a location. We may also get involved in the actual shoot itself. For example, we might be contacted for a type of airplane that needs to be in the shoot, so we've appeared in several movies where aircraft is required.

We were in one of the Die Hard movies when they were filming somewhere up in North America. For those of you who have seen the movie, you may recall the Boeing 747 departing during a significant winter snowstorm.

A little backstory...

The aircraft had arrived from a lengthy maintenance check which included repainting. On arrival, a mechanical issue grounded the plane until the replacement could be flown in and installed. Movies cost a lot to produce and delays to the schedule are costly.

The movie was *Die Hard 2: Die Harder* with Bruce Willis, and the setting was the Washington Dulles airport at Christmas.

We managed to get into the airport, despite difficult, inclement weather. The Airport Authority succeeded in clearing the runway just enough for us to land.

As we touched down, we didn't even realize that we were part of the film shoot. The footage ended up being perfect because there was snow coming down, which was precisely what the director wanted. All on cue.

When it comes to transporting animals, we act only as the conveyance section of the equation. Take racehorses, for example. Racehorses are big business, so when you're moving these beautiful creatures, all the veterinary certificates are handled professionally and must be absolutely up to date. The thoroughbreds have been to their vets, declared fit for travel, and all jabs are current. They're looked after better than small children. These horses never leave the trainer's arms.

When the horses are loaded on the airplanes, there's a special section for them, so there are two in each pen. At the back of the airplane, there are seats for the handlers that travel with them, so they can observe and make sure the conditions are perfect during the flight.

The horses don't seem to perceive that they are traveling on a plane, apart from take-off and landing. I believe travel may be more taxing and tiring for horses in a regular carrier or truck experiencing heavy traffic because of the frequency of the stop and go.

However, the horses don't know any different once they're up in the air. They're fine. It's been shared that the horses push the call button every now and again when they want to change the movie, but apart from that, they're pretty good. Just kidding!

There was another film we worked on called *Operation Dumbo Drop*. This one was interesting because it involved transporting an elephant. You can look up the film and the elephant's name on the internet if you're curious. Anyway, I got a call from this gentleman. He was shooting the movie in Asia but wanted to use a trained elephant brought up in California.

We moved the elephant on a 747. In fact, I've got a picture of the elephant standing right next to the airplane. It was a case of Jumbo meets the Jumbo.

This elephant was so gentle, really a fantastic animal. The trainer loaded the elephant at about 2:00 in the morning, and I brought my wife and young son to see him off. This elephant was so well trained, a lovable animal, and very much connected to humans. The trainer put on a little show for us. He placed an uncooked egg underneath the animal, and the elephant put his foot down on top of the egg and didn't crack it. That was how well trained he was, so docile.

We had a special container made for the elephant on the plane, and his handlers, of course, went on the flight as well. We've moved a lot of animals over the years. In the earlier part of my career, we transported animals to zoos, not from the jungle to the zoo, but from one zoo to another zoo. I've never been involved with any animals coming from the wild. That would make me feel a bit creepy. We've moved fish too. And foxes. Fish, foxes, you name it.

We've transported tons of passengers from rock stars to philharmonic orchestras. We've moved them all, but mostly it has been just regular people on our flights. We could be taking somebody home because they're about to have a baby or someone traveling to a funeral.

We've carried people after they have passed away. We've done many flights taking the deceased back to Muslim home countries in the Middle East. The main reason for these funeral flights is that the dead must be buried within a specific timeframe under Muslim religious beliefs. So, it's necessary to move very quickly, and the flight is like a timed event.

On one side, you must obtain certificates from the mortuary so the deceased will be allowed on the airplane. But then it's also compulsory to obtain all the clearances from the funeral home at the destination country to get the deceased cargo cleared properly.

We've taken some important people to their final resting place. I always consider it an honor, a real honor to do that.

You just never know what the day will bring, literally and figuratively, but I always like the excitement and complexity. I speak to clients, and I listen. The gift is to negotiate and find a positive, workable solution. Every single day we receive urgent requests.

People come to Le Bas to charter aircraft because the scheduled airlines don't have the seats, or time is of the essence.

Often, it will be about a serious matter.

For our airline and military programs, we might be taking a spare part to a country, and the airport is closed at that time of night. So, we'll work with agents on the ground to keep it open. Of course, we'll have to pay extra fees to get in there, but our clients will usually respond, "No problem. Just do it. Make it happen."

Then we need customs and immigration there. "No problem, we'll get that done." We go to that extra place. I've directly called up government entities at two o'clock in the morning and got them out of bed because we needed to overfly their air space. They've permitted us to do it because what we're flying was that important.

Think about it. That's what we do.

In November 1991, at the start of the first Gulf War, Saddam Hussein ordered the Iraqi army to set the oil wells on fire, which had the makings of a global environmental disaster. The Iraqi army set between 605 and 732 fires to oil wells, storage tanks, and refineries.

Le Bas International had been in existence just under a year. We got a call from a company that was very well-known for legal cases. I remember their yearly calendar, which was quite remarkable. On each of the twelve months through the entire year, they had a photo of disasters that they helped mitigate.

One of their past cases was a tragedy on an oil platform in the North Sea, about one hundred twenty miles northeast of Aberdeen, Scotland. Almost all the crew was killed, 167 men and two crew members from a rescue boat.

Anyway, we got a call from this company asking if we could get them into Kuwait despite the raging oil fires. I was like," Oh, my God."

First, this was a challenging request because there were military curfews, with everything happening in and around the combat zone.

Second, the runway had been bombed, so we couldn't use it to get in there.

We had to think hard about this one.

But we figured it out anyway. First, we got the team into Bahrain in the Middle East using conventional aircraft. Then we contacted one of our vendors in the area that operated a De Havilland Canada DHC-6 Twin Otter, a Canadian STOL, short take-off and landing, utility aircraft, which needs very little space to land. It's very marginal.

We took a group of representatives from the company and their computers into Kuwait. The real reason they were traveling to Kuwait was to meet with the royal parties there at the time. The company needed to explain the situation to the Royal family, government entities, and representatives using a computer model to demonstrate what would happen if the fires weren't put out quickly. They did this so the royals would permit them to bring experienced people in to extinguish the fires.

Permission from the royals was essential to the operation.

Within twenty-four to forty-eight hours of arrival, they had permission to send tactical crews to Kuwait and Iraq to contain and extinguish those oil fires. The company contacted Boots and Coots and Red Adair, the biggest names in well control oil disasters on the planet.

For the Middle East, this was a life-changing event with global ramifications. Nobody could get the negotiating team in there to get permission to contain the fires. We did.

Sometimes our clients don't want to go anywhere. They simply desire the privacy and peace created within the closed space of the airplane. Thus, the flight becomes the primary goal of the charter.

At the beginning and near the end of the calendar year, we do quite a lot of board meetings. Executives get together and go out to their various points worldwide to discuss where they have been in the previous year and where the company might be headed in the next. What's the changing strategy, if any, for the next year? What have we accomplished? Where are we driven for the future? What do we consider potential goals? Meetings at the end of the year are the wrap-up. Where did we succeed? What did we miss? Where should we initiate change? How do we make that happen?

We move financial people around when they have activity with their stocks. Perhaps they have a stock sale scheduled. Maybe they must let a lot of people know, within a brief timeframe, that the stocks are available for sale, what they're going out for, or they have to caution others to slow down and think first.

So absolutely, airplanes are chartered for business meetings and business reasons all the time.

There are many reasons why people reach out for critical charters or complicated charters. Sometimes, the motive is pleasure, a celebratory occasion, or a genuinely off-the-beaten-track event.

What if something is happening on the planet that can only be seen once in fifty years? Or maybe just once in a lifetime?

We like to go one step further and explore the exceptional experience.

We do unique travel all the time. In fact, some of the big hotel chains are organizing tours that use their hotels as a base. We've considered a possible joint "seven wonders of the world tour." This is bucket-list travel. A person wants to go on a safari or journey to someplace that's very hard to get to, or perhaps a destination where the airlines typically don't travel. We discuss unusual destination travel all the time, and we're not talking about log cabins or fishing trips. Some of the most interesting are specific occasion or phenomena trips.

Years ago, we had a company come to us. They wanted an extravagant idea to use as an incentive for their executives. A whole concept that would be a once-in-a-lifetime experience.

So, we planned and priced a movable New Year's Eve — actually, three New Year's Eve parties — but all in one night.

The entire concept was designed with a British Airways Concorde in mind - costing a then whopping $1.2 million. The first celebration would take place in New York. We would then fly to the second strike of midnight in Vancouver, and the final celebration would take place in Hawaii. Again, we would travel to beat the clock.

It didn't go. The quote was way more than the company could afford, but they loved the idea. That's our job to come up with out-of-the-box ideas and solutions.

Auroras and St. Elmo's Fire always fascinate people.

Basically, the spectacle is an electrical front. Scientifically, the sun's rays create charged particles that interact with the Earth's magnetic field, exciting the atmosphere and generating light at the polar regions.

And so, the occurrences can generally best be seen near the northern poles, where the sun's rays hitting the atmosphere causes a shadow effect that appears almost like a curtain descending to the horizon.

But you also can get the same effect in an airplane — St. Elmo's Fire. You can create the same effect when you fly from a positive cloud into a negative cloud or vice versa. The windows of older cockpits used to be made with layers of gold. When you turn on the windscreen defroster, you often generate the same effect because the window is holding a charge. The windows will have this ghostly effect in the cockpit, and you can actually put your hand through it.

The Northern Lights are in the cockpit on the windshield.

Another special event we do like to chase is a solar eclipse!

An eclipse is perhaps not a terribly unusual event. But a person generally watches an eclipse from a stationary place on the planet, and it only lasts for a short time. The eclipse is there and over very, very quickly.

But we've done eclipse flights where we've taken people up in the sky and followed the eclipse.

We followed the path so you can stay in the envelope with the eclipse much longer. In one instance, our clients could track and remain in the eclipse for seven and a half minutes because the airplane was chasing it. So, our passengers could see it clearly and unobstructed in the sky.

In fact, one of our clients sent me a lovely picture years ago of the eclipse in Mexico, taken when the first light appeared like a sun blast. Bang. It was like something out of a *Star Wars* movie, where you just capture it all around, about maybe point zero of a second, then you get this, beam of light.

On the first one we did, we took eighty or ninety people down to Mexico to witness this phenomenon. The gentleman who so very kindly sent me a photograph said it all in his note on the back of the picture: "Thank you very much. Could not have done it without you."

Tracey and Capt. Phil "American Dad" Battaglia—Engineering, test pilot, McDonnell Douglas—in the cokpit of a McDonnell Douglas DC-10-30.

Transcontinental Systems Business card, designed by legendary aircraft photographer Austin Brown. Jersey–Channel Islands was my first registered aviation company.

Tracey standing next to Alpha Jet's N25TC Learjet 25. Ken Haas commented on how my enthusiasm was so tangible it would help me succeed in the United States. Ken was an extraordinary pilot and aviation entrepreneur. Long Beach (LGB), California, 1988.

Zurich headquartered Jet Aviation frequently visited the Long Beach Jet Center shown here. Head of state B727 Executive N727KS—an extremely exquisite aircraft, even by today's standards.

Tracey Deakin

Great American Airways' DC-9-15 N1068T semi taxis into our Long Beach Jet Center facility for passenger disembarkation. The relationship with Great American continued to Le Bas International.

Sept 3 – 16, 1996. Hurricane Hortense's highest winds were 140 MPH leading to 39 fatalities and $158 million due to storm damage. The company nicknamed me "Our man in Aruba." (*Photo Courtesy U.S. National Oceanic and Atmospheric Administration*)

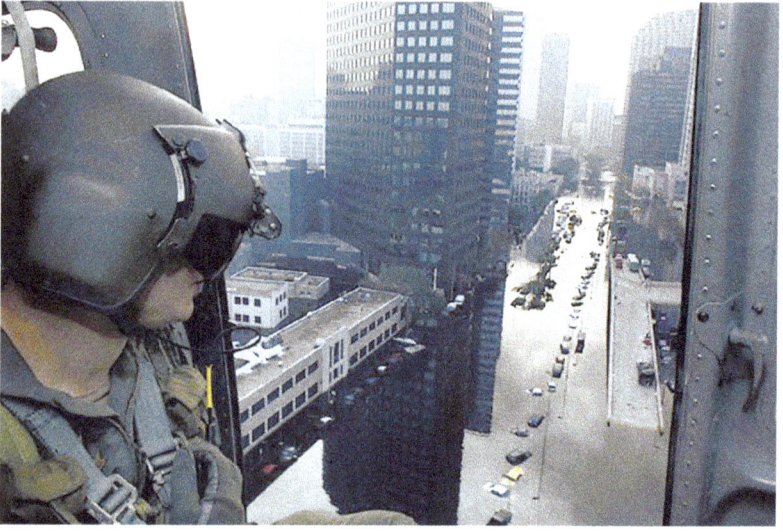

Hurricane Katrina, August 29, 2005 hits New Orleans, Louisiana. The Category 5 Atlantic hurricane caused 1,836 fatalities and damages estimated between $97.4 billion to $145.5 billion. At the time, it was the costliest tropical cyclone on record, the fourth-most intense Atlantic hurricane to make landfall in the contiguous United States, gauged by barometric pressure. Highest winds were 175 MPH. (*Photo Courtesy PixaBay*)

Ariane 5 is an ArianeGroup success story. This heavy-launch vehicle, now retired and replaced by Ariane 6, had a streak of 82 consecutive successful launches. This included the launching of the James Webb Space Telescope (JWST), allowing scientific research and investigation across many fields of astronomy and cosmology to study the observation of the first star, the formation of first galaxies, and detailed atmospheric characterization of potentially habitable exoplanets. Our partnership continues to this day, serving 20 of the world's leading private and government space delivery companies. (*Photo Courtesy ArianeGroup*)

Navy Grumman F-14A Tomcat from Fighter Squadron 114 flying over a burning Kuwaiti oil well. The Kuwait oil fires—a historical, planet-wide catastrophic event—as seen from Space Shuttle Atlantic during mission STS-37. Estimates placed the number of oil well fires from 605 to 732. Circulated news reports at the time argued that some of the effects of the smoke could be similar to the effects of a nuclear winter, with smoke lofting into the stratosphere, a region of the atmosphere beginning around 43,000 feet (13,000 m) above sea level at Kuwait. As it relates to the teams we supported, the final oil fire was capped on November 6, 1991. (*Photo courtesy U.S. Navy*)

CHAPTER 17

Aviation for Art's Sake

"He moves not through distance, but through the ranges of satisfaction that come from hauling himself up into the air with complete and utter control; from knowing himself and knowing his airplane so well that he can come somewhere close to touching, in his own special and solitary way, that thing that is called perfection." — Richard Bach

EVERYTHING WE DO AT Le Bas International is mindful. But, above all, we are personal. I may have an answering service on my private phone, but whenever a client calls one of our communications centers in the United States and Europe, the phone is picked up within three rings. And you speak to somebody who's there to listen . . . a trained professional who can help.

Most people are shocked when they first speak to us, because they're like, "There's somebody there? I'm talking to a real person?" If the client doesn't know us, they may be anxious. But then they realize that they are speaking to a trained professional who is there to help them: "Mrs. Smith, you can expect to pay an average of $43,000.00 on a corporate-sized charter trip." "Mr. Brown, if you require a large commercial airplane, the cost will average between $120,000 to $750,000." Our company respects all clients that are spending that amount of money for that level of service.

We communicate and keep in touch with our customers. At Christmas, we send chocolates. Every quarter, we send out postcards,

"Wish you were here," with a stamp on the card like the old type stickers that you used to see on suitcases. We harken back to the day when people cared about the customer. I think that's the most essential part of the service we provide.

When you lose the trust of a customer, you lose a personal connection.

There is tremendous value in the contact. It's all about using your information to increase your contacts and grow your business. If you forget who the client is, you're done.

As soon as you speak to a person, you're building history. That is something valuable that you should expand and value, just like an old encyclopedia. You put it on the shelf because you never know when you might need it. You want to be able to recall, "What was that company that did this? Who referred us to this client? Who gave us this contact?" If you don't have that historical connection, you lose.

I think the proper word for data is history. That's all it is. And from history, we learn.

We also have the utmost respect for privacy, especially since we often have celebrities or heads of state as clients. These are people in the public domain. Without the public knowing or wanting to know about them, they would just be who they are. I've dealt with so many famous people over the years. The experience is almost like looking into a mirror. Wait, not a mirror, but more like looking beyond a curtain. To get past the curtain and grow to know the real person is difficult. That may come with time, but not necessarily.

In the end, how is that different from getting to know any person? But there is one important distinction.

Within a celebrity, there is a public persona versus a private person. So how do I approach a famous person? No different than you and me talking. That's the pitch. It's just you and me. There is no pitch.

If you're trying to pitch, it's a mistake. You don't do that with anyone.

I tell my staff and myself that an authentic conversation is a coffee conversation.

That's it. It's a "Hey, let's go to coffee. Oh, I understand that you might be interested in airplanes. What fascinates you about airplanes? Well, this is what fascinates me. If you have a moment, I'll explain. But what is it that intrigues you?"

They might answer, "Well, I've got my family member here, and they have to go there." Or, "I've got this piece of equipment over here that needs to be moved."

"Do you use airplanes a lot, or once in a while?" And then I kind of say, "Well, this is what we could do for you. Think about this or think about that." Or, "Hey, if you're up to these many hours, I could do this or add that. Maybe we can offer those, have a look at that for you."

And the reply was usually, "Yeah, why don't you do that for us."

This is no different than any other conversation.

Most of the pitch is listening. That certainly follows along with our whole philosophy of tailoring our level of service to the person's needs.

In today's world, I take my hat off to any artist who is successful because the business is extremely difficult for anybody. For artists to develop from very small humble beginnings to a global presence, they must learn their trade. They've probably played whatever instrument they play since they were five years old. They've been adjusting to it, creating with it. They have studied the instrument they depend on. They went to music school, or acting school. They have practiced ad nauseum, and it is difficult for them to pick up work for a long time.

First, they've not only got to get a version of themselves, their singing, or music out there that they like, but also that people will actually listen to and pay to see. Then they've got to find themselves a manager they can trust, a tour director they can rely on, etc . . .

For an artist to progress from local venues to the world-class performance stage takes time and work. But, once he or she becomes successful, they are an "appetizing" morsel as an entertainer to those who produce and manage them, and of course, to their fans.

It's a necessary evil. He or she has entered the public domain. And without being in the public domain, nobody would know about him or her.

When a musician, artist, actor, singer, or sports figure first breaks into show business and gets known, he or she goes up very quickly. Popularity soars. A song gets launched. A movie premieres. Boom! Everybody wants to see the band, the actor, the singer.

The artist is in demand!

And that's where Le Bas International comes in. Suddenly these artists need air charters. If you think a moment, airplanes aren't just a convenience. Airplanes transport a person from point A to point B as quickly and safely as possible.

Air charter becomes an essential tool. When we start the year, we may be flying some artists around in a very small turboprop. Then, by the end of the year, we're flying them around in a great big commercial airplane.

That's how quickly the process moves, all within the space of a single year.

Lightning speed!

Suddenly, he or she has a schedule. If the performer is on tour, he or she is limited to a fixed number of places they can be during a certain amount of time. If he or she is playing a concert here, somebody may want them over there for an unscheduled appearance. The only way the artist can get there in that compressed window of time is by airplane. So, he or she can go out, play the event, and return to their original schedule.

How this usually works is that the artist has ascended to a point where he or she is getting known, becoming popular, and they're touring. Most travel by tour bus, an average of two to three hundred miles a day from venue to venue.

When putting together a concert, the scheduling is probably done a year in advance. So even if the artist is still relatively minor, he or she can't just turn up and play because somebody may already be scheduled in the concert hall or arena.

Touring puts specific demands on the artist. He or she plug into the cities they're going to, and the question that is constantly being asked is, "Can I get the tour buses there on that date with all the equipment?" It's very stressful.

Let's take an artist's typical day. He will begin at about ten or eleven in the morning. When he is on tour, he'll get to the venue about four in the afternoon. He'll do a soundcheck and make sure that everything is working. Then he goes on stage between eight and ten in the evening.

After the performance, he hosts a "meet and greet" and does everything else like that. Eventually, the performers are back in the tour bus and going to sleep. Meanwhile, all the crew takes down the equipment, and then the entourage travels overnight to the next destination.

The touring schedule is quite brutal. First, the artist is sleeping on a bus, and even if it's a nice bus, it's still a bus. Second, mealtimes are generally before the event, so everyone sits down and tries to have some food before that evening's performance.

When an artist gets super popular, she can only get to so many destinations.

What do you do if you're wanted for an interview on this radio station far away? Or if your agent grabs you a spot on "Saturday Night Live" in New York City? Or if you're invited to Europe for a sponsoring station? Or if somebody wants to pay you a boatload of money to play at their private event?

That's when the artist needs to get to that event and get back to the tour in a hurry. Usually, the artist will work around the tour date and try to get out and return with the least amount of fanfare possible. That's why many television interviews and performances are recorded during the day. They're not really at night like they appear to be. They're recorded during the day so performers can hit and run then continue with their regular schedule.

That's where we at Le Bas come in! We arrange the travel between an unexpected opportunity and the performances that are already scheduled.

The artist will be able to appear on *Good Morning America*, or the BBC, or the French radio during the day. We'll get them in and out and back on the stage for the next performance.

On tour, it is quite common to get a day off between every four or five working days. Sometimes a day off is scheduled, but sometimes not, for example, the booked venue dates are no longer available in consecutive order. So, the planned tour day now becomes an unscheduled day off. If the artist is in demand, he or she likely will go and do something else.

Now, you can't or shouldn't cancel a tour date and say to thousands of people that you are not turning up as planned. If the artist is very well known, a legend, some fans will travel from Australia to Frankfurt just to see them. Many fans will pay $2,000, $3,000, $4,000, or a couple of thousand Euros to see that unique artist because they may only play live once or twice. Serious business!

Artists start using charter airplanes around the point when they have audiences of about 17,000 people. A typical venue can cost anywhere from $1.2 to $1.9 million. And that's just the venue. Then they've got the price of food and drinks. Then, finally, they've got salaries for the crew, and there is always other extraneous stuff. But that's the basic start figure.

On top of that, they've got the equipment. All the massive bands will have two complete sets when traveling, so they'll leapfrog. One set of equipment will play in a major city such as Frankfurt. Then, the band will spoke and hub: From their base of operations, they'll go to a town, play, go back to their base. Then they'll go to the second town, play, and go back again.

While that's happening, the second truck of equipment will leapfrog ahead of them to the next venue and set up the gear. Then while that one's packing up, the first truck leapfrogs again to the next city. They'll go from Amsterdam to Copenhagen or wherever. Some of the big bands can fill four 747s with their load of equipment.

Tour managers have so many factors to consider. There's accounting. There are attorneys who travel with them all the time. Management and touring concerns have evolved since my days with Jerry Bron. They are very professional nowadays with liability considerations, insurance, and everything else.

What happens if the artist is sick?

That's happened to us. I mean, we've had a large airplane on the ramp numerous times, and the artist got sick. We couldn't move them. The show was canceled.

Is there insurance for that?

Yes, they definitely have insurance for that too.

So, touring and travel becomes a balancing act, with the most important thing being safety, then our professional performance.

Global Reach, Personal Touch remains not only our motto but our gold standard.

We've had some clients who have asked us for something that is below our safety obligations and insurance requirements. We just said, "No, we're not doing it. We can't. I'm sorry, not going to happen."

Often, it's not the client who makes these requests. It's the people behind the client who may not understand or are simply trying to cut costs any way they can. The majority of instances are usually the meddlesome people who may not be as professional as we are. In some other countries, other interests may enter the equation as well.

Call it buckshee.

Again, we stay as far away from that tangled web as possible. We would prefer to walk away. Just because you're a client doesn't mean you'll always be our client.

But we do appreciate the complex, demanding lifestyle.

Think of being up on stage and looking out at all those people who expect a memorable performance. The artist has to gear up to perform on a nightly basis. To come down from that performance mentality must be extremely hard. A live act performing artist is expected to do that day in and day out. Sometimes, people get very nervous before going on stage, yet they are most alive when they're on that stage.

The music business, in one way, is fantastic. Look what it does. Look at the revenue it can generate. Look at the goodwill it creates around the world. But many artists are relatively young when they become famous. After they have gone through the growing-up part and get to who they will become, some of them are brilliant. But there are also those who have gone the other way.

We at Le Bas are honored and privileged to support global artists, both at the height of their careers and in their most unfortunate circumstances. Celebrities are human beings who often give their length and breadth to perform. Unfortunately, I've seen many artists who have gone through a phase where they fell off the wagon at the back end.

We've managed a lot of artists who have unraveled after performances. They are supposed to get on the plane, travel somewhere else, and do it all over again. They come to us because we are waiting for them, and they need help. And they get help.

Most of them come back to themselves in the end, but some artists lose sight of the private person and believe their public persona. That's when they run into trouble. They may cut their hair on their charter flight, forget who or where they are, and be found wandering in a park when they are supposed to be on the plane. We care for our clients no matter the circumstances.

When we move artists around an airport terminal, we choreograph the movement throughout the route. We make sure the way ahead is clear and moving. Yes, famous people generally just walk through the terminal, unbothered and unrecognized. How can that happen?

Typically, you wouldn't even notice most celebrities unless you really know who they are in day-to-day life. If I only knew you from pictures, then saw you walking by, I'd probably recognize you. But only if you were at the forefront of my mind.

An artist becomes part of the public's inner mindset because he or she has got a lot of content out there, just like a movie thing. When a movie comes out, you often see the actors speaking about the part because they really want to highlight the film. And while they're out promoting the movie, that is the most likely time that you might notice them.

But generally, you wouldn't see them at all.

Suppose we are transporting a politician, a musician, an artist, or a sports personality. In that case, he or she is more likely to be recognized if they are associated with a recent event, not simply because of his or her profession as a sports personality or musician or anything. If she has just won Wimbledon, you are going to know about her because you've just seen her accomplish an incredible thing. But eight months down the line, you probably wouldn't recognize her.

Fortunately, I do not have a hall of fame for personalities who I have had to kick off the airplane.

One very well-known artist, extraordinarily talented and well-loved, had big problems with her husband. This gentleman had been on previous flights. This one time, he was vulgar and disrespectful to the cabin attendant. In every way, he was being forward. Overly forward. Also, when the couple and their entourage boarded the airplane, they had quite the stash of happy drugs with them, although we didn't realize this at the time.

We consulted the agent in charge of this performer's group to remind him that we could not let illegal drugs be carried onboard the plane.

And this had happened twice previously. This gentleman also brought firearms onboard. Again, we were like, no, no, no.

Our very last flight for this couple, from New York to Florida, broke the proverbial camel's back. About two hours into the flight, I got a phone call saying that there was a bit of a problem.

I asked, "What happened?"

Apparently, this particular gentleman was in the airplane's restroom lighting up. And the crew knew he was lighting up because the ventilation system was sucking the air from the restroom all the way into the cockpit.

When he came out into the airplane, he had his security guard with him, but he also was carrying a baseball bat. And he was still out of order and very disrespectful to the cabin attendant.

So, I got a call. So, we said, "We have had this conversation before and the safety of the crew at the end of the flight is paramount." Luckily the captain of the airplane was a part-time sheriff who was incredible. We communicated, pinpointed the plane's exact location, and decided to put the aircraft on the ground for the safety of the crew and the rest of the passengers.

The person in question was out of it and being rude to the cabin attendant and the crew. The captain was polite and apologetic as he announced a slight mechanical problem on the plane, and it was necessary to land.

Once we had the airplane on the ground, there was a limousine waiting to take the disruptive passenger to his destination. The captain approached the belligerent man and said, "Sir, I'm actually a part-time sheriff. I suggest you get in the car and go. Otherwise, I'm going to have to call somebody else to help."

And the celebrity's husband left.

We handle such situations as quietly and discreetly as possible. Privacy is essential, and we never want anything to get in the media. But subsequently, we haven't done any additional work for them.

Live performances can produce such an emotional roller-coaster. On one of Live Nation's corporate offices lobby walls, there is a massive image of the artist's view of the crowd from the stage. Even if you're not the artist, the image will blow you away. Being up on stage and looking out at all those people. Imagine the performance high you have to climb to on a nightly basis and coming down from that must be extremely hard.

That's the day-in-and-day-out life of a performing artist.

CHAPTER 18

The Future is Bright

"Aeronautics was neither an industry nor a science. It was a miracle." —Igor Sikorsky

THINK OF WHERE WE'VE come in the last hundred years in aviation, the last fifty years, the last twenty-five years, and then look forward. I have adjusted my angle from aviation towards aerospace because I see opportunity.

Every single day I look at it. It's probably my dyslexic brain because, with everything I face, I see all the possibilities at once. My brain lights up, and I go for the big picture. I say, "Oh, why can't we just do this as opposed to this?" That's the way I look at stuff now. I think of that beautiful shot of the Pan Am shuttle joining the space station in *2001: A Space Odyssey*. That is coming.

We have served clients who have ventured beyond earth, and we continue to be part of their courageous journey. I believe that we're destined for elsewhere in the future. I see the interest in commercial space travel growing with different enterprises involved: Virgin Galactic, Blue Origin, United Space Alliance, NASA. India just put a rocket up recently. If we were to join all together, we could be much further along than we are now.

Hiccups are apparent within the aerospace industry, partly because companies are getting too big and their efforts too segmented. And so, communication is impaired. Everybody is speaking, but not everyone is listening. They're all seeing these words fly backward and forwards, but they are not really digesting the meaning.

Instead of somebody asking the hard questions, "By the way, did we really look at that? Is that the right way forward? Have we spoken to the customer about that? Is that acceptable?" They just say, "Hey, this is what you are doing." But they don't think the process all the way through.

As an industry, we are getting blowback in light of the Green New Deal mentality to reduce greenhouse gas emissions, but that's a good thing because it makes people think. It forces the industry to improve and change. A lot of companies now are burning a different type of fuel that is less polluting. It's like cars. Remember that people used to fill diesel cars with oil from the chip pans? I used to drive up behind them. They smelled like a burger joint.

Critics say that aviation pollutes the planet. Well, yes, it does pollute. But if you consider where it's come from, where it was, the miles traveled, you may have a different perspective.

Does it make sense to use an airplane to go an hour and a half?

If you think about that, driving would be better and more cost-effective, especially if the car is electric. But if you go to the airport, wait all that time for your flight, travel there, check your bags, go through security, and everything else, that will probably take four hours to complete an hour and a half travel time. That doesn't make sense.

But if you're traveling across the country, or a distance that would be more than three hours of car travel, then airplanes are the most cost-effective and non-polluting means of travel in relation to the environment.

Air travel is getting better and quieter. We're developing electric airplanes. So, in response to the environment and climate change, an evolutional transformation is already in play.

The biggest polluters on the planet are in the marine business, specifically cargo boats and cruise ships that pollute way more than anything else. The amount of carbon tonnage they put out on all those big vessels is ginormous, a fact that is only just coming to light.

Statistically air travel is much safer than travel by car. And with the advent of autonomous planes, it's going to become safer still. I fully believe that electrically powered vehicles, whether cars, trucks, or airplanes, are the way of the future. Of course, there will be hiccups along the road, as with everything, but it will be done right.

Perhaps blowback isn't the word that I should use unless blowback means "change."

I think blowback implies "evolution." It's all very well saying blowback, but we must think forward. Everything changes. The improvements and new technology will be developed and mastered.

If you come close to Earth, the younger generation is very comfortable with autonomous vehicles. I'm pleased with autonomous, and the car I have is nearly self-driving and will be more so very soon. But, as my wife says, I prefer how you drive compared with the car. I say, "Thank you very much." But the autonomous vehicle is no different then when somebody else drives your car.

Autonomous airplanes have been around for a long time, both in space and close to the Earth. We call them drones. Autonomous planes are coming, though this is not to say pilots won't be needed any longer. Still, an autonomous world will have a lot of positives and a lot of negatives.

What's good is that we are technologically advanced enough to support an autonomous airplane. Think of the commuter train at an airport. You get on a train to go to different terminals. It's safe, and you have no problem getting on it and riding. Everybody boards it. It's just a way of doing business now, and the train leaves on time. When you get on the train, a warning sounds, the doors close, and off it goes.

Imagine what that concept is going to do for commercial aviation. There's no question. If you get on the airplane, guess what? You'll have a warning, the doors will close, and it will depart. The plane will not wait for you. It will be gone.

If you consider computerization, the good thing about artificial intelligence (AI) will be that it will separate airplanes. You will not have weather problems because it will be autonomous. Yes, fierce storms will still cause a problem as such, but autonomous-wise you can keep all the aircraft separate, just like the autonomous cars on the road now keeps the vehicles separate. So why couldn't the controlling AI do that in the air?

Our business will play towards that autonomous model in years to come, autonomous electric airplanes, absolutely, because of the increased efficiency. Why wouldn't we as long as it will be safe? I don't know of any drones that have suggested that the model is inherently unsafe. I haven't seen anything military-wise apart from tests that have gone wrong. So, a lot of the argument confirms they will be safe in the future.

I have some definite ideas about improving airport design. There will not be any parking because there will be no need for a parking lot. People will be dropped off at the airport by their autonomous cars.

There will be no need for a check-in desk. Drop your bag, and the machine will scan your identification. Put your bag on the conveyor and, it will pass through the scanner, be tagged, and loaded onto the airplane. Walk through security and you will be in the terminal. You will self-screen, and your phone will inform you where to board the aircraft. The doors will close, the take-off will be on time, and the arrival as well.

There will be no need for mass terminals with shops. You will just be departing or arriving. What do you need a shop for? You are there to get from departure A to arrival B. Shops slow everything down. We only need coffee shops in terminals because when the airplanes are delayed, we need something to eat.

Think about it. We have pubs, bars, and restaurants because we're waiting for something to happen. However, the entire experience can be made a lot more efficient. If you put it under a microscope, the result would be well-organized and effective.

Airplanes were originally made from cloth. What happened to the seamstresses and the people who made the cloth that wove the fabric? Then, we used metal on the fuselage of the airplane. Now, scientists and engineers are developing 3D printing airplanes. You need those specialists. The labor-intensive stuff maybe not so much, but new technical employment opportunities will be required.

Progress moves skills forward.

Jobs won't disappear. They'll just evolve into the next technology, but we will always require and expect a standard of service. We are humans, after all.

A company out of Tel Aviv called Eviation is developing an all-electric nine-seat regional aircraft called the *Alice* that is designed to fly 440 nautical miles on an 8,300-lb. battery pack. The aircraft, which is powered by two MagniX electric motors, has already been ordered by Boston-based Cape Air. The Eviation *Alice*, the world's first all-electric passenger and cargo plane, took its first flight on September 27, 2002, at the Grant County International Airport in Washington. The flight lasted eight minutes, with the plane ascending to 3,500 feet powered by Siemens electric engines.

The electric airplane will have so much power. I have an electric car now, and they're unbelievable. When you put your foot on the accelerator, you lose your lunch. This plane is designed to keep flying even if it loses one engine because it has that much power. Since it is electric, it is also clean, light, blends in at night, and requires only a two-crew operation.

When commuting between smaller cities, the plane's projected costs will be about $200 an hour to operate. That is nothing. The revolution is here. This plane has already taken off.

At present, the biggest challenge is batteries.

But the search is on for lighter materials to use in the manufacture of batteries that allow for maximum energy storage. The way forward is through storage supplies, whether a gel or something similar. The race is on to make the batteries lighter and more robust.

Instead of having fuel in the tanks, an electric composite will be in the tanks that holds charged energy, similar to Tesla cars.

What's the word again? Future.

We must abandon the gas and oil mentality and embrace a new paradigm of green design. It's not a question of if we get off fossil fuels, but when. If you look around, anything that's plastic should be redesigned. Anything that's made from fuel-based and oil-based material must be restructured.

Since it was first developed, we have been fixated on plastic, but to environmentally disastrous ends. We are finding plastic trash in the deepest part of the ocean. Scientists recovered shrimp from the depths. When dissected, they found small traces of plastic in them. So that means the plastic trash is sinking.

A young inventor in Europe has come up with a self-driving machine that sucks up the plastic trash in the ocean like a giant filter vacuum. We've got to clean up our mess, and that will demand a transition of thought. We must be willing to consider the necessary adaptations.

For every negative, we must look at the future. I believe a negative can often become a positive. A negative begs important questions: "What can we do to change that? How will it change our lives? Will it save lives? Can it make things better for us as human beings?"

Altering a negative to a positive takes a bit of practice. Whenever I encounter a negative, I keep at it until I answer the questions and produce a positive. For example, when I have a customer we haven't had for quite a while, I will work with this customer until I win them back. That persistence is in my DNA. Giving up is not me as a person or us as Le Bas International. That's not what we're about. If you give up on something, then you're the fall.

Backed by a watch company, a group of aviation enthusiasts in the UK has totally rebuilt an eighty-year-old Silver Spitfire from scratch. They rebuilt it from top to bottom, re-did the whole engine, like new. So, the plane does have a modern machine, and they're flying it.

The Spitfire, initially meant to only fly for forty-five minutes at a time, is now flying around the world. The Spitfire and its engine, the Rolls Royce Merlin, represents freedom the world over.

I suppose it's like the P-51 Mustang or Harley Davidson here in

America. What do they really symbolize for America? Freedom. In England, the Spitfire means the same thing. It's part of our identity. Logistically magical and much loved.

I get more and more inspired by stuff like this. When I was younger, I liked the nitty-gritty, but now my brain is screaming, "Forget the nitty-gritty! Let the younger people do the nitty-gritty, and you direct them. You're the orchestra leader, get on and do the things that count!"

I can still see the path before us very clearly now, like one of those Indian summer moments that I remember so well when I knew which type of aircraft was descending by their sound. The power was back, a whoosh of the engines, vibration of the air coming past the engines at the back.

When you fly in the evening, everything seems to be organized. You can imagine it yourself when you look out of an airplane as the sun is going down, and people seem to be quieter at that time of day. The world suddenly seems to make sense.

As human beings, you look up into space, and you see that is where we've done something good. We've got to keep going and do better. Think of all the technological advantages we've made and how they've collided with our history. Without aerospace, we wouldn't be where we are.

England is a great place, my native country, but I embrace a global view of the world because of my travels, because of my work. Every single country on the planet brings something to the international landscape. What is good about the United Kingdom is its history. But I can also say the same for China and India and every country. They all have a history behind them, and that account of the past works to develop the future.

England is a bit stuck in their ways, snobby I would say is the word. But then I translated that to the United States. The United States is the melting pot of the world, but if you were to put America, the EU, and other countries all together in a big swirling pot, the ideas that would come out of that would be breathtaking and humongous.

What America has is capitalism. But if capitalism is taken too far, it becomes exploitative and greedy. It's just like when you go into a candy store. If you have everything in the candy store, you get bored with it, instead of picking up what you really want. If we all work together, can you imagine what could be done? It would be unbelievable.

As I travel around the world, not just in the United Kingdom or the United States, I see lots of these tiny ideas coming up. Beautiful things are happening in some places in Africa, but they don't have the funding to bring the ideas to fruition. I do not propose simply throwing money at something, but I'm talking about developing projects that actually work and change lives.

The difference between the United Kingdom and the United States is that the United Kingdom is a cottage industry, for lack of a better word. If you go back to the Second World War, the British Empire was huge, expansive because of what it accomplished. But today, it's more like a cottage industry doing great, fantastic stuff, but in some ways, holding itself back.

America is more like the wild west; anything goes, which is kind of good. I think if the two countries would find a midway in between, a balance, then it would be perfect. That's where we'll discover leadership for our future.

Introducing *Alice*—aviation's electrification of the future: https://www.eviation.com/ (*Photo courtesy Eviation*)

Alice: State-of-the-art design, 260 knots maximum operating speed, 250 nautical mile VFR range. Accommodations for commercial or executive use, including cargo configuration with a cabin width of 6ft 4in (1.93m) and height of 4ft 11in (1.5 m), useful payload 2,500lbs. (*Photo courtesy Eviation*)

Tailor-Made to Fly

CHAPTER 19

The Light that Shines

"To most people, the sky is the limit. To Those who love aviation, the sky is home." — Jerry Crawford

A S A CHILD, I sat enthralled watching this grainy image of Neil Armstrong and Buzz Aldrin get out of the lunar module and step down onto the surface of the moon. I was awed and inspired as I listened to the crackling of the audio transmission, and yes, it was a giant leap for mankind.

Many years later, I was fortunate enough to have the opportunity to interview Buzz Aldrin. What struck me most when speaking to Buzz was his will to move beyond his accomplishment with his sights on the future. He seemed a little bit frustrated that we have failed to continue our journey to space and beyond as human beings. With all the money and resources that were spent on space and technology, it was one of those times when the country stopped short, when everything got behind. What made the lunar program and the International Space Station (ISS) happen was the Russians. The whole country united together, and we ended up on the moon.

He was frustrated that we hadn't done anything since then. We hadn't been back to the lunar environment, and we didn't have any plans to do anything else, to explore further. NASA with the Space Shuttle was a great idea, and no question putting a space station in earth's orbit was a good move. But he felt like we were just fiddling around with the space program instead of really accomplishing something and moving forward to the next step.

According to Buzz, we failed because we did not have a concrete mission.

At least, that was what I heard in his voice. When you're communicating with busy people, just like myself, you have to be tactful, open, and give value for return. This is what I do. I just keep knocking at the door. You cannot stop. You must be persistent.

It's just like Gulfstream. I spoke with them recently, because it's one company that we don't yet service.

Their representative said, "I have to apologize. I just haven't had time to connect with the right people, but I hear you're expensive."

I replied, "Where did that come from? We've never quoted you." So, I told this gentleman, "You know, we just recently transported components for a broken airplane to a Gulfstream client." Then I changed the direction of the conversation and said, "I actually have to tell you something else. I've met Allen Paulson."

He immediately perked and said, "What? How?" Suddenly, we were having a coffee conversation. He was super interested because Allen Paulson was an American businessman who transformed Gulfstream Aerospace into the world's biggest producer of business jets.

I explained, "Well, I used to be on the board of the Aero Club of Southern California."

My association with the Aero Club does open doors for conversation. Still, it has also been truly rewarding to me personally.

Founded in 1908, the Aero Club of Southern California has remained true to its undertaking throughout its long history. The club's primary purpose has always been to introduce and educate the public about the technology of flight. A non-profit organization, the club is run by volunteer officers and board members. I had the privilege of serving on the board from 1991-1996, and more specifically, I administered the scholarship program.

The club offers generous scholarships for young kids interested in aviation or aerospace higher education. I remember the very first speech I did for them was in the dome in Long Beach where Howard Hughes's Spruce Goose used to be hangared. Underneath the wings of the historic Spruce Goose, there were all these tables set up. One big, long table at the top was raised above the others, and some significant aerospace world leaders were present. When they had asked me to speak, I was nonchalant and accepted right away. I said, "Of course, I've spoken before."

Then that night, I couldn't believe how jittery in the stomach I felt. Actually, let me back up a bit.

Mike Whitman introduced me to the club, and when I was asked to be on the board, I was honored to serve.

About this same time, the Spruce Goose was the center of controversy because the site where it was stored was being sold. So, you could say the plane was being evicted.

Moving the historic aircraft to a new home stirred a hornet's nest of different opinions. Various museums wanted the aircraft, but they planned to break it into smaller pieces. They were interested in housing the cockpit but were not interested in the rest of the plane. They were going to take it apart as salvage and sell the wood.

The Aero Club did a great thing when they gathered several commercial exhibitors to prevent the Spruce Goose from being destroyed. They were able to exhibit it in the dome at Long Beach, over next to the Queen Mary.

When the dome was closed in 1992, the Aero Club helped find another investor, Dale Smith from Evergreen Airlines, who brought the Spruce Goose to an aviation history museum in McMinnville, Oregon, where it remains today.

So, back to the scholarship dinner.

On this particular night, when we were doing this, I told the group about the value and importance of good aviation mechanics. "People don't realize how important mechanics are," I said, "Without mechanics manufacturing and repairing, airplanes wouldn't exist."

Jumping up to 2019, SkyWest here in San Luis Obispo opened up a maintenance facility. When they ran an ad for maintenance people, they needed fifty to fill their positions. Guess how many applicants showed up for interviews?

Zero.

In fact, many airlines cannot now service routes because they don't have enough mechanics to keep the airplanes maintained and repaired. As a result, mechanics are becoming prestigious jobs again.

I was very honored to administer the Aero Club scholarships. However, as I toured the aviation colleges in California, I was surprised by the amount of paperwork and meetings required to get the school faculty to send students to us.

People forget that if you don't have a product, bricks and mortar, that you can sell and that the customers are interested in buying, you will in no way have engineers. But then you need engineers to make the products, so the customers get interested. So, we're back to the importance of finding a balance somewhere in the middle.

The Aero Club of Southern California also honors outstanding achievements in the aviation and aerospace industry with the prestigious Howard Hughes Memorial Award. Since 1978, a medallion, cast in solid silver from Hughes' Nevada mines, has been given to a single individual for lifetime achievement in the field.

The Howard Hughes Memorial trophy is a globe and vehicle sculpture engraved with all recipients' names on the base. The list reads like a Who's Who in the aviation and aerospace industry.

At the meetings, I was fortunate enough to be involved with people from all walks of life who will be remembered and honored as giants in the aviation and aerospace industry.

For example, at one meeting, I found myself talking to the gentleman who flew the Spruce Goose with Howard Hughes himself. He was pretty matter of fact about the whole experience.

To him, it was just his job.

Quite often in life, you do these things, and you don't really value it at the time. To this gentleman, he was just working on the airplane. He was the co-pilot in the seat when Howard Hughes got the damn thing in the air. And that's history.

He didn't think it was going to happen. He just thought they were doing taxi trials. So, he never thought it was going to be in the air. But then Hughes just turned the massive aircraft around, put the power all the way up, and went for it.

I suppose it's kind of nice being touched by giants: Scotty Miller who was the Aero Club president then, was actually tied in with Air Force One, and Clay Lacy. I have an extensive relationship with Clay Lacy, founder and chairman of Clay Lacy Aviation. I've been using Clay's airplanes for eons. So, there's a lot of people in the club that you just got to know.

I think of my conversations with them. When you're speaking to people who have excelled in their careers, exchanging information, and sharing details backward and forward, that is how everybody learns. I hope to see some of the scholarship recipients receiving the award someday.

At the expert level, Aviation gets to be a small world. People can learn and have meaningful conversations. The Aero Club of Southern California is an incredible organization that has been in existence for a long time and has accomplished some really great things. It's no wonder that the giants in the industry want to be associated with it.

One year, the award went to one of the Tuskegee Airmen. I had a long chat with this gentleman and remembered him saying that aviation was something he just wanted to do. But, like most people who made a difference, they didn't realize what they were doing at the time. That's not bad. That's good.

They're not driven by a goal but by a love of aviation. A passion that becomes their goal. They just happened to be really good at what they do and progress bit by bit, and that was how they became giants.

Because of aviation, I've been all over the world. But in my early career, I visited my sister, who was living in Norway at the time, and I was very taken aback by the Norwegian culture and their way of thinking. It's funny, they're an amazing bunch of people, but I think they still have their Viking touch about them.

At first, I found the Norwegians were not very communicative. They just pass you by in the street, and they don't say anything. The younger generation is definitely changing. You can see the global influence.

But at the time, I found that once you got invited into their houses or went out somewhere with them, they were quite different. When they're out, they drink like fish. I mean, a vodka bottle is gone. So, they're entirely different, but they're beautiful people.

I was very much taken by the country, very much taken by their ethics. Perhaps all countries have their flavors, no matter if it's in Africa, or if it's in India, or Scandinavia, or the United States. But in the United Kingdom, I think it's challenging for younger generations to move on if you're not from the elite.

Now, Scandinavia, to me, has everything figured out when it comes to social medicine and looking after elderly people. They educate their kids from a very young age. They let them grow where they want to grow. They don't funnel them and such.

But one of the best things that I love about them is how they celebrate Christmas, like most of Europe, on the evening of the 24th. In Oslo, where I was visiting, there is a sculpture park called Vigeland Park. Right next to it is a very large cemetery, and it's always snowing there in the winter.

On Christmas Eve, before the Norwegians go and celebrate, all the families visit the graveyards to honor and remember their past relatives. They bring these twenty-four-hour candles with them, placing them next to the graves. Then as they go on to their church services and celebrations, these candles continue to burn, descending in the melted snow. The whole graveyard looks like Times Square or Trafalgar Square, with those beautiful candles radiating out from the frozen whiteness.

I think of all the aviators who created an industry, a way of travel and life where nothing existed before. I remember the light that shines from all their successes, failures, trials, and achievements. They are glowing not from inside the snow, but from the sky.

In closing, I share my wish for you to follow your individual passion and enjoy the journey of life.

About the Author

B ORN IN THE UNITED KINGDOM and educated at Bethany School, Goudhurst, Kent, Tracey Deakin has a lifelong fascination with aviation and aerospace.

Tracey's passion for the industry brought him to his first job in aviation at Invicta International in 1976. Shortly thereafter, he attained his pilot's license.

With a career spanning more than five decades, Tracey's efforts with Invicta, IAS Cargo Airlines, El Al Israeli Airlines, and Zambia Airways formed the building blocks to support interactions with major domestic, European, and International air travel.

In 1987, Tracey arrived in the United States and helped launch Alpha Jet, Inc. as well as the Long Beach Jet Center in the burgeoning air charter and corporate aircraft business.

Tracey Deakin is one of the original founders of Le Bas International, an air charter company synonymous with providing excellence to a global clientele.

About the Co-Author

D AWN C. CROUCH FIRST crossed paths with Tracey Deakin after learning of Le Bas International's heroic efforts to evacuate refugees after Hurricane Katrina.

She asked Mr. Deakin to write a testimonial for her first novel, *Against The Wind*, based on her family's experience in the storm.

Mr. Deakin graciously agreed and the two formed a friendship that produced *Tailor Made to Fly*: *Life Lessons in Custom Charter Aviation*.

A native of New Orleans, Mrs. Crouch is a former dancer with Houston Ballet. She writes fiction as well as the popular *Garage Ballet* series, instructional booklets peppered with stories from her life as both dancer and teacher.

www.hellgatepress.com